On Course T

On Course Together

The Churches' Ministry
in the
Maritime World Today

by

BILL DOWN

General Secretary
of The Missions to Seamen

THE CANTERBURY PRESS NORWICH

*The Canterbury Press Norwich, St Mary's Works,
St Mary's Plain, Norwich, Norfolk NR3 3BH*

*The Canterbury Press Norwich is a publishing imprint
of Hymns Ancient & Modern Limited*

A CIP catalogue record for this book
is available from the British Library.

Cover design by Richard Morgan

ISBN 1 85311 007 8

First published 1989

© *Bill Down*

Photoset in Great Britain by
Rowland Phototypesetting Limited, Bury St Edmunds, Suffolk
and printed by St Edmundsbury Press Limited,
Bury St Edmunds, Suffolk

Contents

In 1984, I accepted an invitation to become President of The Missions to Seamen, the Society which is the Anglican Communion's outreach to the seafaring world. During my Installation Service, Canon Bill Down, the Society's General Secretary, spoke briefly of its origin in the 19th Century. He told of the early seamen's chaplains and lay workers, describing them as "men of faith and love, courage and vision" who "made a great contribution to improving the life and working conditions of seafarers".

Since 1984, I have visited more than 25 seafarers' centres in all parts of the world, some more than once. I have seen at first hand how The Missions to Seamen and other church-based Societies carry out their ministry to the seafaring community of the 1980's. The words which were used to describe their 19th Century forbears can still be used of the chaplains and lay workers whom I have met.

In no sphere is their vision more evident than in the development of ecumenical collaboration. In the ministry to seafarers the Churches are not rivals but partners.

Canon Bill Down is uniquely qualified to trace the story of how the Churches have come together to serve seafarers. He has brought to this task a detailed knowledge of his subject, much of it gained at first hand. But more than this, he has brought an infectious joy in, and enthusiasm for, everything which is encompassed in the words 'a ministry to seafarers'.

It is my earnest wish that this book will increase knowledge of a fascinating branch of the Church's witness and work in the world. May it be an inspiration to all who seek to transform the visions of unity into reality.

Anne

Preface by the Archbishop of Canterbury

I am very grateful to Bill Down for this encouraging account of maritime ministry today. Seafarers are well used to uncertainty and change. This book does not dodge the pressures they face. It illustrates the necessity of a consistent and integrated Christian ministry to the seafaring community.

I am glad to read how ecumenical cooperation has flourished within maritime ministry. Bill Down enthusiastically describes and evaluates the work of many agencies other than those sponsored by the Anglican Church. The coordinating role of the International Christian Maritime Association receives his whole-hearted support. It may well be that it is in special circumstances, such as those of maritime ministry, that practical ecumenical progress is most likely to be achieved. Other examples may be found within the Prisoner of War camps in the 1940s, or within China in recent decades. But this account of ecumenical cooperation in Christian mission challenges us to see how such cooperation might be achieved more generally.

Maritime ministry contains another general lesson. The wide variety of cultures, languages and traditions represented amongst seafarers makes it the easier to recognize the unique character of each pastoral encounter. The versatility required of the maritime minister is one which is becoming equally necessary in the multi-cultural communities of our cities and towns on dry land.

I commend this book warmly because of its important implications for Christian ministry in general. But it is also a most enjoyable and readable account of maritime ministry in itself. I know that very many people, all over the world, join me in expressing my appreciation of The Missions to Seamen and all that the Society has done to build the Kingdom of God amongst seafarers.

Robert Cantuar

Dedication

On Course Together, which was a labour of love, is dedicated to the wonderful band of Christians of all traditions who joyfully and faithfully serve the Lord among the seafarers of the world. It was their vision of inter-confessional partnership and their whole-hearted commitment to collaboration which provided the material about which I have written. It was their unfailing kindness, friendship and fellowship which encouraged me to try to record the significant events of the past twenty five years in the sphere of maritime ministry. And it is a tribute to two of them now rejoicing upon another shore and in a greater light, Monsignor Francis Frayne of the Apostleship of the Sea and Prebendary Tom Kerfoot of The Missions to Seamen, who, when the Churches gloriously came together in maritime ministry, were the right people in the right place at the right time.

Acknowledgments

There are a great many people to whom I am very grateful for their help and encouragement as I wrote "On Course Together", and I would like to express my thanks to them all.

The Chairmen of the major committees of The Missions to Seamen—Viscount Leathers of Purfleet, Mr. David Newbigging, Bishop Dennis Hawker, Mr. Ian Campbell and Captain Peter Doble—were most understanding and kind in granting me three months sabbatical leave in which to undertake the necessary research and begin writing. My fellow Executive Secretaries in the Central Office of The Missions to Seamen —Glyn Jones, John Barker, Gillian Ennis, David Hardy, Richard Mulkern and Patrick Ritchie—willingly and very ably covered my duties during my absence. My Personal Assistant in the Central Office, Rhos Charles, has been superb: she typed the whole manuscript (most of it several times), undertook detailed research on a number of subjects, and mastered the mysteries of a word processor as she went along. Her colleague Diane Cox gave her great help and support.

Many friends and colleagues of other organisations and different ecclesiastical traditions went to great trouble to dig into archives, supply information and offer advice. Among them were The Revd. David Harries, Principal Chaplain of the British Sailors' Society, and his colleague, The Revd. Richard Edwards; The Revd. Bernard Krug, General Secretary of The International Maritime Association; The Revd. Dr. Roald Kverndal, Executive Secretary of the International Council of Seamen's Agencies; Lt. Cdr. Richard Frampton, General Secretary of the Marine Society; The Revd. Johannes Aardal, formerly General Secretary of the Norwegian Seamen's Mission; Monsignor John O'Shea, of the Pontifical Commission for the Pastoral Care of Migrants and Itinerant People; Mr. Bernard Clampton, Secretary of the Royal National Mission to Deep Sea Fishermen, Canon Christopher Hill, the Archbishop of Canterbury's Secretary for Ecumenical Affairs; Captain Wim Kuijper, Master Mariner; The Revd. Jacob Schokking; and Captain Henry Severs, Master Mariner.

Among the many books and papers to which I referred I found invaluable help in Roald Kverndal's "Seamen's Missions: Their Origin and Early Growth", Peter Anson's "The Church and the Sailor", Ewan Corlett's "The Ship: The Revolution in Merchant Shipping 1950–1980", and Adrian Hastings' "A History of English Christianity 1920–1985". A separate bibliography of some of the other works to which I referred is included elsewhere.

The publication of *On Course Together* has been made possible by a most generous grant from the Marine Society. The encouragement and support I have received from the General Secretary, Richard Frampton, and the members of the Council has been heartwarming.

I am grateful to the following individuals and publishers who generously permitted the use of copyright material. They include The Society of Authors, as the literary representative of the Estate of John Masefield together with Macmillan – New York 'Sea Fever' from *The Poems* by John Masefield (1953), '*The Church and the Sailor*' by Peter Anson, Burns & Oates, England, Dr Roald Kverndal from his major work '*Seamen's Missions: Their Origin and Early Growth. A contribution to the history of the Church Maritime*' and New English Bible © 1970 by permission of Oxford and Cambridge University Presses. I am grateful to the Institute of London Underwriters for permission to use the table of Casualty Returns.

A number of friends very kindly read various sections and gave me invaluable help and advice. Among them were Rear Admiral John Barker, The Revd. Dr. Paul Chapman, Captain Peter Doble, Dr. George Emmons, Mrs. Gillian Ennis, The Revd. David Harries, Bishop Dennis Hawker, Mr. Peter Johnson, The Revd. Bernard Krug, Mr. Richard Mulkern, Mr. David Newbigging, Monsignor John O'Shea, Captain Henry Severs and The Revd. Dr. James Whittemore.

My greatest debt of gratitude is to my wife Sally. She has been my constant companion, support and inspiration throughout my twenty five years service with The Missions to Seamen. She encouraged me to write "On Course Together", and the three months I spent at home working on it in her company as she studied for a Diploma in Religious Studies was wonderfully satisfying. She has been a tower of strength to our family and managed our home magnificently in my frequent absences.

Introduction

For the last twenty five years it has been my privilege to serve God in the ministry of His Church among the seafarers of the world as a member of the staff of The (Anglican) Missions to Seamen. They have been happy and rewarding years.

From the middle of 1963 until the end of 1974 I served as a port chaplain in South Shields, Hull and Fremantle (Western Australia), and for brief spells in emergencies in Belfast and London. During those years I visited more than 10,000 ships, served as a chaplain in the Royal Australian Naval Reserve, went to sea on a number of short trips, and sailed from Fremantle to Tilbury on a container ship, the "Discovery Bay", of Overseas Containers Limited.

In 1975, after a year as Deputy General Secretary, I became General Secretary of The Missions to Seamen, and in the years since then I have visited most of the major ports and many of the seafarers' centres operated by the Churches and by secular organisations throughout the world. I have met many wonderful people among the seafarers and those who serve them. I have been privileged to meet many leading people in the Churches and in the shipping world. I have experienced great joy and satisfaction in the ministry to which God called me, and I have come to see that we who serve God in the maritime ministry of the Churches have much of value to share with our fellow Christians and with the world at large.

I decided to write "On Course Together" for a number of reasons. The first was that the quarter of a century in which I have served with The Missions to Seamen has been a time of revolutionary change, both on the shipping scene and in maritime ministry, and I felt that the time had come to take stock of what has happened. The second was that in these years inter-confessional collaboration in maritime ministry has grown from a small shoot into a great tree bearing good fruit, and I felt that what has been achieved was of enormous value to the Churches individually, and to the Church as a whole. I also felt that somebody who had been intimately involved in the process of change both as a chaplain in various ports and also in the joint decision-making of ecclesiastical partnerships should attempt to record what has happened and put it in perspective. The third was that the two people best qualified to undertake this task, Monsignor Francis Frayne, of the Pontifical Commission for the Pastoral Care of Migrants and Itinerant People, and Prebendary Tom Kerfoot, my predecessor as General Secretary of The Missions to Seamen and the first General Secretary of the International Christian Maritime Association, both died before they could tackle it. With their passing it seemed to me that as the one to whom Tom Kerfoot had passed his mantle in The Missions to Seamen nearly thirteen years ago I had at least been involved—perhaps as much as anybody else in the Churches—with all the changes and developments, and that it was right for me to do it myself. The fourth was that I wanted to do it!

Once having decided to write "On Course Together" I worked out what I would try to achieve. I set out to paint a picture of seafaring both in the past and now. I aimed to put the maritime ministry of the Churches in perspective by sketching the main events and factors which have influenced its development in the last two hundred years and analysing the current shipping scene. I determined to try to outline the main characteristics of maritime ministry today, and to place on record the remarkable story of the establishment of the International Christian Maritime Association and its growth in importance and influence. I decided to portray the richness and diversity of current maritime ministry by describing ten widely different ministries representing different Christian organisations and various parts of the world. Finally I set out to identify the contribution maritime ministry might make to the life of the Churches and indicate how it may develop in the future.

Any mistakes of fact or errors of judgement are entirely my responsibility—though I have done my best to avoid them —and I apologise in advance for them. If "On Course Together" helps anybody to a fuller understanding of the Churches' ministry to seafarers it will have achieved its purpose.

Bill Down
St. Michael Paternoster Royal, September 1988

On Course Together

I The Sea, The Seafarer and The Church

'They that go down to the sea in ships,
    and occupy their business in great waters;
These men see the works of the Lord,
    and his wonders in the deep.'
                    Psalm 107, verses 23 and 24.

Throughout history the sea has stirred the spirits and imaginations of people living by its shores and far beyond.

To the casual observer it is beautiful, majestic, endlessly fascinating—and sometimes terrifying. To the artist, poet and musician it is a source of inspiration. To the young it represents joy and happiness. To the amateur sailor keen to test his skill and courage against its uncertain moods it is an eternal challenge. To the angler and swimmer it is a source of sport and recreation. To the busy city dweller taking a break from work it promises relaxation.

To the seafarer and fisherman it is their livelihood, to be treated with respect and awe as well as professional skill. To maritime nations it is both a uniting bond of trade, commerce and culture and a natural barrier against predatory rivals. To the diver its underwater life is a source of never-failing surprises and wonder. To the lifeboatman, lifesaver and coast-guard it is something to be treated with caution and un-relenting vigilance. To the marine architect the design and construction of ships able to withstand any dangers it can offer is a continuing challenge. To the shipowner it represents business, trade, employment and a satisfying life. To the Christian it is part of God's creation: He made it, He sustains it, and He cares about the people involved with it.

The sea can raise the human spirit to the highest peaks of exaltation, and it can strike terror into the innermost depths of our being.

The sea has always been important for mankind. From earliest times it was a major source of food. Men and women used their ingenuity to catch fish and other sea creatures to eat. They soon discovered what was edible and what was not, and learned to utilise the non-edible parts for domestic and trading purposes.

It was important for trade. Very early on there was great demand for sea products, such as fresh fish, preserved fish, fish oil, fish skin, fish glue, the meat of sea creatures like the turtle and octopus, and salt. Pearls, shells and brilliantly coloured coral were highly prized. Boat building developed. Communications were established between people living far apart. Small rafts, canoes, catamarans and boats made from reeds, skins or wood were used in shallow waters, and bigger craft were built for deep water fishing and carrying passengers and cargo. Chieftains and traders operated fleets of fishing and trading vessels and built jetties and harbours to accommodate them. When valuable natural resources were discovered in various parts of the world bigger craft were designed and built to transport them. When people began to travel more extensively it became necessary to provide simple living accommodation on board for them. The sea was often the only medium for trade and travel.

It was important too for acquiring and defending territory and property. Human nature has changed very little through the centuries. There have always been nations, communities and individuals who could not be content with what they already possessed but must add as much as they could to it—by force if necessary. As trading developed the aggressive side of man's character manifested itself. Boats were built for attacking purposes. Piracy became a problem. In self defence nations, communities and individuals built similar vessels. The emergence of Navies was an inevitable product of man's aggressive and acquisitive spirit.

The people who sailed on ships from earliest times until the end of the nineteenth century and even beyond led tough lives. Most of them were men. Often they lived in primitive conditions. Furniture and equipment were minimal. Food was of poor quality, without variety and in poor condition. Fruit and fresh vegetables lasted only a few days into a long voyage.

Adequate provision of fresh water was always a problem. Disease, was widespread.[1] The work was very demanding.

Towards the middle of the nineteenth century the introduction of the iron-hulled steam-powered ship marked the beginning of a revolution in ship design, construction and propulsion. By the end of the century it was apparent that the steam ship was fast replacing the sailing ship on most of the world's trading routes, though the transition took many years. For the seafarer the new ships represented the beginning of improved accommodation and conditions of service on board. The changes were warmly welcomed.

But while ships have developed, and living and working conditions on board have improved out of all recognition, the human element of seafaring has changed very little. In every age certain basic features of life at sea have been apparent: they manifest themselves in different ways at different times in different people, but in essence they remain the same. It is important to identify them if the Church is to minister effectively to seafarers.

Life at sea can be lonely. A seafarer may be away from home for long periods of time. In the present century it was quite common until the 1960's for seafarers to be away for two years, and it is still the case today that some seafarers from developing countries spend well over a year away from home. Regular prolonged absences can have a disturbing effect both on the seafarer's quality of life and on that of his family.

Loneliness can be a problem for the seafarer. He or she is cut off from home, family and friends. If he is married he misses out on whole areas of family life, such as his children's growth and development, and unrepeatable family occasions. He misses his friends in the local community. He has nobody on board to whom he can relate in the same way that he does to his wife and family. He may not have a friend on board with whom he can discuss the things that really matter to him. He is surrounded by the same people day after day for weeks and maybe months on end, and he may not particularly like them. He looks forward to his shore leave, but even that too can be frustrating, since both he and all the family know that his leave is limited and that his absence rather than his presence is the norm. Going away for the next voyage gets harder with the passing of the years.

Unmarried seafarers experience a different sort of loneliness. Young seafarers on their first voyage often find the loneliness almost overwhelming, and a significant number leave the sea during the first year. Long term unmarried seafarers often adapt well to life at sea, though they too find parting from home, family and friends painful. Some homosexual seafarers establish relationships with other homosexuals: these relationships often become very intense and their fears of separation and loneliness are very real. And seafarers whose marriages are in trouble or have broken up often carry an extra burden of loneliness. The chronic loneliness of the seafarer is a constant factor of life at sea.

Life at sea can be boring. Out of sight of land one stretch of water looks very much like another. The people on board are the same every day. When the voyage ahead is a long one, and progress seems slow, time drags by. The routine of shipboard life becomes monotonous. Counting the days already spent at sea becomes counter-productive. Using the hours off watch constructively can be a problem for the seafarer who is not an avid reader, skilful with his hands or a particularly sociable person.

In the days of sailing ships seamen dreaded the days when there was no wind and no headway was made. Time passed slowly, everybody became irritable, and only a spark was needed to ignite and inflame smouldering irritations, dislikes and resentments. Extremes of climate accentuated the problems caused by boredom. Hot weather made people lethargic and short-tempered: cold weather made the business of keeping warm and dry an overriding concern. Boredom is something every seafarer experiences.

Life at sea can be frustrating. By the nature of their work seafarers are cut off from shore life for long periods of time, and this can bring its problems. Sailing ships often waited many days for a favourable wind to set them on their way; indeed, it was seeing a huge fleet of vessels at anchor for many days in Penarth Roads in 1835 which inspired the pioneer of The Missions to Seamen, The Revd. Dr. John Ashley, to leave parish life in order to minister to seafarers in the Bristol Channel. The waiting was tedious. Today ships arriving at a port sometimes have to wait until a suitable berth becomes available before they can load or discharge their cargo. The seafarer on board can see life going on normally ashore, he is looking forward to a change of scene and stretching his legs, but he has got to wait for this until the ship berths. Extremes of climate can make the waiting which has always been part of the seafarer's life—waiting for orders, waiting for the weather to change, waiting for disputes to be resolved, waiting for shoreside formalities to be completed—even more difficult to tolerate. And the unceasing movement and noise of a ship at sea can make constructive use of leisure time difficult; his attempt to write a letter home when his ship is rolling, pitching or vibrating can lead a seaman's wife to question the sobriety of her husband at the time he was putting pen to paper!

On shore the seafarer may face different frustrations. He may not understand or speak the language of the country he is visiting. He may dislike the local food and drink. He may not be familiar with local customs or culture. He knows that if he does not speak the local language and is obviously a stranger some local traders will do their best to part him from as much of his money as they can. And he must endure the hurtful and grossly exaggerated reputation that has traditionally branded seafarers the world over as drunks, womanisers, gamblers and ne'er-do-wells. The fact that the majority of seafarers are normal ordinary people whose behaviour is usually unexceptional is frequently ignored by people who have never understood the tensions and anxieties of a seafarer's life and judge them all on the basis of their observation of a minority.

Life at sea can be dangerous. It has always been so and it still is. Natural hazards include fog, squalls, storms, freak waves, shoals, reefs, hidden rocks and unpredictable currents. In polar waters icebergs and freezing seas are a menace; constant vigilance must be exercised to prevent heavy layers of ice forming on masts and superstructure and making the ship topheavy and liable to capsize. In very hot weather there is always a risk of fire. The movement of a ship can often spell danger to the seafarer; in rough weather it can be difficult to keep steady on his feet, work safely on the open deck, carry out delicate jobs in the engine room, and even get into or out of his bed. In the age of sailing ships adjusting the sails in stormy weather was a nightmare.

There are human hazards too. They include faulty design of ships, faulty stowage of cargo, poorly maintained navigational aids, lack of necessary information, inadequately maintained equipment like lifeboats and liferafts, failure to ensure that all officers and senior personnel are properly qualified, and the mental and physical fatigue which can lead to carelessness. Serious illness at sea out of reach of skilled medical attention is an ever-present concern. The presence of pirates, who will stop at nothing to seize valuable cargo, is an additional source of anxiety in some waters.

In every age ships have regularly been lost at sea. When ships sink or are lost in other ways the lives of seafarers are at risk. Even in the 1980's more than 150 ships of 500 or more gross registered tons are lost every year for one reason or another.[2]

Ashore the dangers are different. There have always been people lying in wait in port areas for the seafarer with money in his pocket. The stranger is fair game. There have also often been gangs of one sort or another whose aim is to exploit the seafarer. From early times, and legally in Britain from 1556 till the middle of the nineteenth century, 'impressment' into the service of a nation's Navy in times of war was common practice. The notorious 'Press Gangs' (groups of naval officers and seamen sent out into port towns and the surrounding countryside to round up seafarers for enforced service in the Navy) were hated and feared by merchant seafarers everywhere.

Crimping was the name given to a long-running racket in which organised groups of ships' agents, representatives of unworthy shipowners and rogues of both sexes joined forces to persuade seafarers to leave their ships in foreign ports before the legal completion of their voyages and thereby forfeit all their accrued wages. The devices they employed included offers of attractive, well-paid—but non-existent—jobs ashore, straight cash payments, the delights of settling ashore with beautiful women whose characters changed dramatically on the departure of the ship, and other subterfuges. The hardness of the seafarer's life at the time rendered such propositions initially very attractive to him, but once hooked and landed, his money gone and his wages forfeited, he was abandoned to his own devices. He had no means of getting home and often became further indebted to the crimps, who would get him another ship—for a commission, of course! An early form of this evil practice, dating back to the seventeenth century, had the crimps plying the seafarer with enormous quantities of liquor until he became totally intoxicated and oblivious to everything; they then delivered him, for payment of an agreed price, to the Press Gang.

The dangers ashore for the seafarer of today are different but real. Dockside bars harbour thieves. Brothels carry the risk of deadly infections. Muggers abound in some ports. Drug pushers are constantly on the lookout for potential carriers of parcels of addictive drugs. Political police in some countries pounce on seafarers passing unwise or injudicious comments.

Another regular feature of seafaring which profoundly affects the seafarer's life at sea is the element of uncertainty of employment. In times of prosperity and war there have always been plenty of jobs for seafarers—sometimes more jobs than there were seafarers to fill them—but because of the uncertainties and irregularities of both trade and of life at sea most seafarers were traditionally employed on a voyage by voyage basis. They sought new employment wherever and whenever it was available after paying off and taking leave. In times of recession unemployment was a haunting, unwelcome and ever-present spectre. In the twentieth century the influence of trade unions has revolutionised conditions of service for seafarers from industrialised countries, but the current practice of registering ships under flags of convenience[3] and employing seafarers from developing countries at much lower rates of pay has sharply re-introduced the element of uncertainty of employment. Seafaring is a specialised work, and abandoning it to seek employment ashore can be a painful process.

While life at sea can be lonely, boring, frustrating, dangerous and uncertain, it should also be said clearly and unequivocally that it can be wonderfully satisfying. Through the centuries countless seafarers have found it so.

It is exciting to visit new places, catch a glimpse of different cultures, sample interesting and unfamiliar food and drink and meet people of other countries. It is exhilarating to experience the sea in its infinite variety and to pit knowledge, experience, skill and courage against the elements. It is inspiring to observe the beauty and the majesty of the sea, and to see how the challenges of seafaring can bring out the best in a person.

It is good too to be part of a well-run ship, to be trusted and relied on as being thoroughly competent in a particular job, to be part of a team or an organisation carrying valuable and much needed cargo from one part of the world to another, and to make deep and lasting friendships with people of different countries, cultures, races, languages and faiths. It is very satisfying, too, to be an integral part of the great brotherhood of the sea: it is an intangible, unarticulated, but very real, bond linking seafarers of all races, ranks and creeds in spontaneous willing help to fellow seafarers in trouble or danger.

These are the features of seafaring which basically do not change. But other aspects of it are constantly changing. The shipping world is a complex one. Many diverse interests are involved. Uncertainties of cargo, trade, money, weather and communication are ever present. Designs of ships change. Patterns of trade change. New commodities appear on world markets. Wars occur. Political alignments change.

In this as in every setting the Church is called to proclaim the Good News of Jesus Christ for all people.

Jesus gave the Church a clear mandate for its ministry to seafarers. He chose a port city, Capernaum, as His home and the base for much of His public ministry. He chose fishermen to be among His closest followers. He called Peter to be the rock on which He would build the Church. He stilled the raging of the wind and sea and calmed the fears of His terrified followers in the waterlogged boat.[4] He came to His disciples walking over the waters of the sea and invited Simon Peter to walk across to Him.[5] He showed them that the sea, like all of Creation, was subservient to God. When He told His disciples to go into all the world and make disciples of all nations, baptize people everywhere, and teach them to obey His commandments, He surely had it in mind that His servants would travel far and wide and that some of that travel would be by sea. Witness to seafarers would be an integral part of their mission and ministry.

In the early days of the Church St. Paul travelled extensively to preach the Gospel. He often faced danger at sea.[6] Once he was adrift on the open sea for twenty-four hours.[7] He was shipwrecked three times.[8] When the ship carrying him to his trial in Rome was wrecked on the coast of Malta he displayed a strong faith and cool composure among a group of men who

were physically, mentally and spiritually exhausted after fourteen terrible days and nights in a small ship in a fierce storm
and having had little sleep or food. His was a telling and
impressive witness. And the care of the Maltese for the shipwrecked crew provides one of the earliest recorded examples
of practical ministry to seafarers: 'The rough islanders,' St.
Luke tells us,[9] 'treated us with uncommon kindness: because it
was cold and had started to rain, they lit a bonfire and made us
all welcome.' Just as Christian travellers and seafarers could be
wonderful ambassadors for Jesus, so Christian people ashore
could offer a ministry of welcome, love and witness.

In the early centuries of the life of the Church records of
active ministry among the seafaring community are rare but
not totally absent. In 563 or thereabouts St. Columba set out
by sea from Ireland to carry the Gospel across the waters. He
established a religious community in Iona in the Inner Heb-
rides, from where he and his companions evangelised the
surrounding islands and the mainland. Their boats were small
and frail, but the monks were intrepid sailors.[10] In 651 a priest
called Utta was despatched by Oswy, King of Northumbria, to
escort his bride-to-be on a voyage from Kent. It is recorded
that in a severe storm Utta poured holy oil on the waters to
calm them.[11] The first known English naval chaplain[12] was
Odo, who served in the Saxon fleet of King Athelstan in the
tenth century. He later became Archbishop of Canterbury and
died in 959. Around the year 1000 a priest accompanied the
Norse explorer Leif Erikson on a voyage to the North American continent.[13] In 1147 a large expedition set sail from
Dartmouth in England bound for Lisbon to fight against the
Moors. It was decreed that on board each ship there should be
'a priest, and the same observances as in parishes on shore'.[14]
During the Crusades, which took place at various times between 1095 and 1464, Franciscan friars, priests and monks
sailed on the ships with the Crusaders, sharing the life and
privations of the seafarers.[15] Priests and monks sailed on ships
carrying pilgrims to shrines in Europe and the Holy Land, and
in the Age of Discovery (the late fifteenth century) priests sailed
on the Portuguese and Spanish galleons. They sought to
establish the Church wherever they went and at the same time
ministered to the seafarers.[16]

In the centuries before the printed word was widespread the

Church supported seafarers in a number of ways. Prayers were said at the launching of new vessels and when seafarers joined a ship. Hermits spent their lives on treacherous shores praying for the 'souls and safety'[17] of seafarers, and tending bells or beacons to warn them of impending danger. Monasteries in port towns and cities sometimes provided sanctuary and treatment for sick and injured seafarers. And in a number of ports confraternities of seafarers (like Trinity House in London) were established. Trinity House, a guild of 'shipmen and mariners of England', was set up in 1517 by King Henry VIII 'to the praise and honour of the most glorious and individable Trinity' to do all things necessary 'for the relief, increase and augmentation of the shipping of this our realm of England'.[18]

With the division of the Western Church at the Reformation in the first half of the sixteenth century distinct Roman Catholic and Protestant traditions emerged, and it will be useful to trace briefly the development of maritime ministry in each.

In the Roman Catholic Church in Reformation and early post Reformation times three great saints set glorious examples for future ministry to seafarers. St. Francis Xavier (1506–1552), ordained priest in 1537, sailed from Lisbon in 1541 in the galleon 'Santiago' to evangelise the East Indies. 'Conditions on board were little better than those on a slave ship. St. Francis devoted himself unceasingly to his shipmates . . . himself caring for those who were ill. He heard confessions, taught Christian doctrine, and was loved by all because of his great cheerfulness . . .'[19] He has been described as 'one of the greatest of Christian missionaries',[20] and 'the patron of Catholic action afloat'.[21] St. Vincent de Paul (1580–1660) also experienced life at sea at first hand. While on the short voyage from Marseilles to Narbonne he was captured by pirates and sold to a fisherman in Tunis as a slave. Constant seasickness severely restricted his usefulness at sea, and he eventually escaped and returned to France. In 1618, under Louis XIII, he became Captain of the Galleys, and was responsible both for improving conditions for the slaves and also for making available to them the ministry of the Church. His 'Rules for Sea Apostles' included instructions not only for moral and religious affairs but also for dealing with acts of abuse and injustice on board the galleys. He has been described as 'the patron of Port Chaplains and others who engage in the Sea Apostolate on shore'.[22] St. Peter Claver (1581–1654) obeyed a call to serve in the New World and in 1610 sailed for the Caribbean and North South America. Ordained priest in 1616 he devoted his ministry particularly but not exclusively to the care of the galley slaves. He described himself as 'the slave of the Negroes for ever'.

During the two centuries after the death of St. Vincent de Paul in 1660, and despite the examples of such saintly men and the devoted ministries among seafarers of many ordained and lay people in coastal parishes, monasteries and chantries, the Roman Catholic Church was slow to develop and co-ordinate its apostolate to seafarers. However, in the second half of the nineteenth century, when the full impact of the Industrial Revolution was being felt in Britain and Europe, and communications between nations by land and sea were speeding up, the beginnings of the international outreach of the Roman Catholic Church's ministry to seafarers can be discerned. In 1922 the Pope formally approved and gave his blessing to the newly established Apostleship of the Sea—the outreach of the Roman Catholic Church to the seafarers of the world—and a very important and influential new dimension was added to maritime ministry.

In the Reformed Churches, as in the Roman Catholic Church, the years between the beginning of the Reformation in the first half of the sixteenth century and the end of the eighteenth century saw many fine Christians, lay and ordained, individually making a great impact on those areas of the shipping scene with which they came into contact.

In 1553 the Governor of the Company of Merchant Adventurers, Sebastian Cabot, gave instructions to his captains that the services of Morning and Evening Prayer were to be read daily on every ship. In 1626 King Charles the First of England gave orders that chaplains should sail on all his ships, though many years passed before this became any kind of reality. In 1653 public worship of God was made mandatory in ships of the British Navy. In the seventeenth century three English non-conformist ministers—John Flavel in Dartmouth, and John Rhyther and James Janeway in London—exercised fruitful and widely acclaimed ministries among seafarers. The eighteenth century—the age in England of 'the sleepy

Anglican Church, the sleepy and unlearned universities, the rosy fox-hunting squires, and the top-booted hard-drinking legislators at Westminster'[23],—was not notable for any comparable ministers, but it did produce some fine Christian seafarers. John Newton, who was once a slave-ship captain, became a Church of England priest and wrote some well known and much loved hymns, including 'Amazing Grace,' 'Glorious things of Thee are spoken' and 'How sweet the name of Jesus sounds.' A major influence in his life was another shipmaster, Captain Clunie of Stepney, a true 'seafaring shepherd of souls.'[24] In North America a Quaker seaman and later shipowner, Captain Paul Cuffee, the son of an African slave father and American Indian mother, was renowned for the strong Christian character of his ships' crews. He led by example.

Tracts and devotional manuals for seafarers were written, produced and distributed in England, North America, Germany, Holland and Scandinavia in the eighteenth century, and another form of ministry to seafarers was initiated by the English 'Society for the Propagation of the Gospel', which in 1701 instructed its missionaries proceeding to appointments overseas to minister to the passengers and seafarers on board the ships on which they travelled. But, as in the Roman Catholic Church at the same time, there was no organised ministry to seafarers in the Reformed Churches. Indeed in many ports there was no ministry to seafarers at all.

In the Reformed Churches this situation changed at the beginning of the nineteenth century. The change began almost simultaneously in England and the United States of America.

In England the way had been prepared by a religious and humanitarian revival in the second half of the eighteenth century in which the preaching of John Wesley and the newly formed Methodist Church were key factors. At the beginning of the nineteenth century an important and influential group of Christians known as the 'Clapham Sect' were campaigning strongly for social reform. William Wilberforce (1759–1833) was deeply involved in the crusade to abolish slavery, and the 'Cambridge Evangelists', among whom Charles Simeon played a leading role, were key figures in the Evangelical Revival which swept across the country.

Seafaring was much in the minds of English people at that

time for a number of reasons. Captain Cook's voyages of exploration and discovery had caught the public imagination. There had been a long and wearying succession of wars at sea. There was growing public hostility to the evils of slavery and the slave trade, and in the Churches the call to proclaim the Gospel throughout the world was being taken very seriously.

The establishment of Christian ministry among seafarers was a natural outcome of the attitude of the Reformed Churches in England at that time, and the first half of the nineteenth century witnessed the birth of many new ventures in this field. Their origins and development will be briefly portrayed in Chapters Two and Three.

In the United States of America at the same time there was a similar rapid and widespread development of ministry to seafarers. George Whitfield's great preaching ministry there in the 1740's had led to a religious awakening, and in the early years of the nineteenth century exciting ministries among seafarers were pioneered. Their origins and development, together with those of the Nordic and German missions to seafarers, will also be traced briefly in Chapters Two and Three.

Notes

1. During the Armada campaign in 1588 the 'Elizabeth Jonas', an English ship, lost 40% of her crew through sickness. In Sir Francis Drake's voyage of 1585–6 to the West Indies almost 600 men out of a total of 2300 died from disease. See 'The Sea Chaplains', by Gordon Taylor, published by the Oxford University Press, p. 51.

2. The Institute of London Underwriters published the following statistics concerning Total Losses, including Constructive Losses, of ships of 500 tons gross or more:
1982—236 ships; 1983—209 ships; 1984—214 ships
1985—188 ships; 1986—156 ships; 1987—112 ships.
The gross registered tonnage of a ship is the measure of its internal volume.

3. By the term 'flag of convenience' is understood the practice of registering a ship in a country other than the one in which it is owned. This is often done to obtain more favourable taxation concessions, or to avoid the stringent safety standards of the country of ownership, or to escape the attentions of trade unions over conditions of employment.

4. St. Matthew, Chapter 8, verses 23–27.

5. St. Matthew, Chapter 14, verses 25–33.

6. St. Paul's Second Epistle to the Corinthians, Chapter 11, verse 27.

7. Ibid. verse 25.

8. Ibid. verse 25.

9. The Acts of the Apostles, Chapter 28, verse 2.

10. 'The Church and the Sailor' by Peter Anson, published by the Catholic Book Club in 1948, p. 11.

11. 'The Sea Chaplains', by Gordon Taylor, p. 1.

12. 'Seamen's Missions: Their Origins and Early Growth' by Roald Kverndal, published by William Carey Library (California) 1986, p. 6.

13. Ibid. p. 6.

14. Ibid. p. 6.

15. Ibid. p. 6.

16. Ibid. p. 6.

17. Ibid. p. 15.

18. From the original constitution of Trinity House as quoted in the Oxford Companion to Ships and the Sea, published by the Oxford University Press, 1976.

19. 'The Church and the Sailor' Peter Anson, p. 27.

20. Oxford Dictionary of the Christian Church, published by the Oxford University Press.

21. 'The Church and the Sailor' Peter Anson, p. 27.

22. Ibid. p. 27.

23. 'A History of Europe, from the beginning of the 18th century to 1937' by H. A. L. Fisher, published by Eyre and Spottiswoode p. 704.

24. 'Seamen's Missions: Their Origin and Early Growth' by Roald Kverndal, p. 9.

II The Beginnings of Organised Ministry to Seafarers

'There is perhaps no order of men upon whom the labour of an intelligent clergyman could be bestowed with greater prospect of success than on seamen.'

Archdeacon John Owen[1]

It was at the beginning of the nineteenth century that the Reformed Churches in Britain and the United States of America heard a clear call to establish ministry to seafarers on a more comprehensive and concerted basis. In both countries the religious awakenings of the second half of the eighteenth century had led the Churches to undertake programmes of evangelism, outreach and social and moral reform. The development of maritime ministry and the pioneering of organised missions to seamen in the two countries show striking similarities and took place at virtually the same time, and it is necessary to trace their growth and expansion in both places and throughout the world in order to understand and assess today's maritime ministry. Because the theme of this book is the Church's ministry to seafarers now and in the future rather than in the past the emphasis of this historical sketch will be placed on highlighting important events and trends rather than supplying exhaustive detail.

1800–1860

'I must go down to the seas again, to the lonely sea and the sky,
And all I ask is a tall ship and a star to steer her by,
And the wheel's kick and the wind's song and the white sails shaking.'

John Masefield, 'Sea Fever'

'No man will be a sailor who has contrivance enough to get
    himself into a jail; for being in a ship is being in a jail, with
    the chance of being drowned . . . a man in jail has more
    room, better food and commonly better company . . .'
                                                    Samuel Johnson[2]

The purpose of the juxtaposition of the two quotations
above is to contrast a popular romantic view of seafaring with
its harsh realities in the period under review, which was the
heyday of the wooden-hulled sailing ship.

In the newly-established United States of America a vast
ship-building programme was under way at the beginning of
the century to cope with a great expansion of trade to the Far
East and elsewhere and to compete with other trading nations.
By 1800 its register of deep-sea ships exceeded half a million
tons[3] and the number of seafarers registered between 1796
and 1812 was in the region of 140,000.[4]

In Europe at the beginning of the century Britain was at war
with France. The outcome was decisively influenced by a
number of great battles at sea in which huge fleets of men-of-
war of various types were involved, and the British naval and
merchant fleets were manned at that time by more than a
quarter of a million seamen.[5] The slave trade was flourishing,
with up to 100,000 people enslaved each year. The Industrial
Revolution was in full swing, and the development of the
steam engine in the latter part of the eighteenth century was
destined to change the face of shipping by the end of the
nineteenth. In 1802 a steam-powered stern paddle vessel, the
'Charlotte Dundas',[6] started a towage service in the Forth and
Clyde Canal, but another half century passed before further
refinements in steam propulsion seriously undermined the
dominance of the sailing ship. Other countries with important
merchant fleets at that time included France, Portugal, Spain
and The Netherlands.

For the seafarers manning the sailing ships of those days life
was hard. Their accommodation was sparsely furnished and
lacking in comfort. The crew slept, ate and lived in the
forecastle, which was usually dark, poorly ventilated, cramped
and damp. Extremes of climate and the uneven motion of the
vessel exacerbated the discomfort. The smell produced by a
combination of damp clothing, sea-sickness, stale food and

unwashed bodies was highly unpleasant. The food was monotonous and often in poor condition because of the difficulties involved in storing it for any length of time. The drinking water was often far from fresh. Fevers, viral infections, skin disorders, malnutrition and contagious diseases like tuberculosis were common. Mental disorders were widespread.[7] The work was physically demanding and often dangerous— climbing the masts or rigging to adjust the sails in pitch darkness at the height of a storm with cold wet hands, while trying desperately to cling to slippery spars as the ship rolled, pitched or tossed, was a hazardous business, and many seafarers plunged to their deaths. A significant number of ships sank in storms. In unheated accommodation it was often impossible to get clothes dry for days on end, and exhausted seafarers slept in their hammocks in sodden clothes. In opposite extremes of climate, when the wind failed and the ship was becalmed, time passed slowly. Frustration mounted steadily, tempers became frayed, and trouble was never far away. Over and above these daily privations, rigours and dangers, the discipline on board was harsh; the Captain was absolute master of his ship, and often the crew and even some of the officers lived in terror of him. Small wonder then that seafarers looked forward eagerly to getting into port and going ashore —the prospect of a break from routine, of seeing new faces, eating different food, sampling local drinks, enjoying female company and visiting new places had a great appeal.

Ashore in foreign countries, with money in his pocket and a longing to enjoy a brief respite from shipboard life, a seafarer could easily find himself in trouble. In every major port of the world, then as now, there were people waiting eagerly to part him from his hard-earned wages. In dockside bars all manner of cheap and heady liquors were sold, and thieves and pickpockets hung about until a likely victim was sufficiently intoxicated to be robbed with impunity. Prostitutes, as always, were a regular feature of dock areas. So were traders in goods of dubious value. And as in every generation there were organised gangs methodically exploiting the weak points of the shipping industry.

One racket which flourished in many ports virtually throughout the nineteenth century was 'crimping', described briefly in Chapter One. Roald Kverndal describes it vividly in his book 'Seamen's Missions: Their Origin and Early Growth':

> 'The crimping system was destined . . . to rank as the most notorious international impediment to the spiritual and social welfare of seamen. By the 1820's the crimp was already only too well established on the British waterfront as a species of seaport parasite whose sole profession was to separate the sailor from his hard-earned wages by fair means or foul, normally foul. His method consisted in attaching himself to his victim from the earliest possible moment, and thereupon exploiting every peculiarity of the seaman's situation and character to serve his mercenary end. For this purpose the crimp would organise a whole hierarchy of helpers. Himself often a wealthy publican or boarding-house owner he would be in league with 'runners', 'brothel keepers', 'pot house bullies', 'cheating slop sellers',* and 'pettyfogging sea-lawyers'. With their aid the crimp would establish a virtual monopoly in meeting those two basic needs of any home-coming seafarer—relief from the privations and stress of sea life, and re-employment when no longer willing or able to remain at sea.
>
> The resultant system of 'marine slavery' seemed completely fool-proof. By devious means the seaman was duly fleeced both of what he had earned on his arrival and of any advance (generally two months wages) obtainable on his departure. Meanwhile the crimp cunningly contrived to make the shipowner dependent on him for supplying new hands when and where needed.'[8]

It was estimated that in the 1820's there were at least 50,000 persons involved in crimping on 'the North bank of the Thames alone. It was a racket prevalent in many of the major ports of the world, and the description of crimps as 'land sharks' and 'soul sellers' (from the Dutch word zielverkooper)[9] seems eminently appropriate.

Another was the Press Gang, also previously mentioned. In times of war there was always more demand for seamen to man the Navy's ships than there were seamen willing to serve

---

* 'slops' are clothes.

in them—mainly because of the extremely rigorous conditions under which naval personnel served, and because flogging was a common punishment. Impressment into the Navies of many countries was common practice. At the beginning of the nineteenth century the war between Britain and France was at its height and British merchant seamen dreaded the consequent impressment.

Such was the seaman's life ashore and afloat at the beginning of the nineteenth century.

In Britain and the United States of America the Reformed Churches perceived a need to minister to these men whose lives were spent on the oceans and whose time ashore was often accompanied by trouble. From small beginnings a movement which was to spread throughout the world steadily gathered momentum.

In Britain the Naval and Military Bible Society was founded in 1779 to provide Bibles for distribution among naval personnel 'in order . . . to spread abroad Christian knowledge and reformation of manners'.[10] Its early work was undoubtedly an influence in the religious awakening which took place in the Royal Navy in the subsequent wars with France. The Marine Society, founded in London in 1756, recruited, trained and equipped boys and young men for life at sea. Jonas Hanway, a noted philanthropist, was a key influence in its establishment and early work, and he wrote a number of Christian based manuals of instruction for young seafarers. The appointment of chaplains to serve on board naval vessels had long been a fact of life in the Royal Navy, and some fine priests, among them Dr. Thomas Ken, who became Bishop of Bath and Wells in 1684, served in this capacity. At the beginning of the nineteenth century, however, the number of naval chaplains was small, and some of them made little positive impact on the seamen. But the provision of ministry to seafarers on an organised basis originated in Britain with The Revd. George ('Bosun') Smith (1782–1863).

George Smith went to sea at the age of fourteen as a cabin-boy on an American merchant ship, the 'Betsey'. The ship was intercepted by a British warship, H.M.S. 'Scipio', which was short of crew, and Smith was impressed into naval service. He became ill with yellow fever but recovered and

spent more than five years in the Navy before becoming ill
again and being invalided out. In 1803 he committed his life to
Jesus Christ and four years later was ordained into the ministry
of the Baptist Church at Penzance, where he stayed for eight-
een years. There, in addition to his chapel duties, he preached
and ministered to local fishermen and seamen. As a former
seaman himself he understood their way of life and their needs.

In 1809 he was invited to preach on a Revenue cutter, the
'Dolphin', and as a result of the impact this visit made on him
he set up the Naval Correspondence Mission, with the aim of
encouraging self-examination, study of the Scriptures and
providing specific advice. In 1812 he visited London and
preached a special seafarers' sermon at the Carter Lane Baptist
Chapel. It was a great occasion—large numbers of seafarers
and others were present, the Captain of the Tower Hill press
gang attended, and his sermon made a great impression. The
seeds of Smith's future ministry in London were sown.

A movement which began in London in 1814 also had a
great influence on him. In that year a devout Methodist
shoemaker, Zebedee Rogers, met Captain David Simpson, a
merchant seaman, at the Wesleyan Chapel at Rotherhithe. As
a result of their meeting Rogers visited Captain Simpson's
ship, and a well-attended prayer meeting was held on board.
Encouraged by this Rogers was soon holding prayer meetings
on other ships, and with the help and financial support of a
local Christian timber merchant, Samuel Jennings, the Bethel
movement began. Bethel means 'House of God', and in 1817 a
ship in the Thames raised a hand-made flag with the word
'Bethel' sewn on it to indicate that a prayer meeting was to be
held on board. The idea was an immediate success, and soon
numerous Bethel flags could be seen flying from the mastheads
of merchant vessels all over the world. The Bethel movement
made an enormous contribution to the spiritual life of countless thousands of seafarers in the years ahead, and George
Smith was quick to recognise its potential.

In 1817 he was invited to preach on board the 'Agenoria', a
British vessel moored off Wapping in the port of London. A
huge crowd attended a very moving service, and this led Smith
and others to consider establishing an itinerant preaching
ministry on board merchant ships to supplement the itinerant
prayer meetings of the Bethel movement. In 1818 the 'Port of

London Society for Promoting Religion among Merchant Seamen' was formed,[11] and H.M.S. 'Speedy' was purchased for adaptation as a floating chapel. This new Society aimed to promote the 'religious instruction, moral reformation, and eternal happiness' of seafarers, and was to be 'an intended union of all denominations of Christians', avoiding sectarian views and party feelings. It planned to proclaim the Gospel by preaching and various other means, including the religious instruction of young sea trainees. Today's British Sailors' Society has its roots in this society.

Smith was intimately involved both with the formation of this Society, and also, in the following year, of 'The British and Foreign Seamen's Friend Society and Bethel Union', whose object was 'the promotion of an evangelical union of seamen, supra denominational in basis and supra national in scope.'[12] In 1825 he was the driving force behind the decision to open the London Mariners' Church, and in 1826 he moved to London to become its first minister. He had visionary plans for a marine academy, a seamen's portable library, reading rooms, a seamen's register, a seamen's savings bank, a boarding-house referral system and day schools for the children of seamen and rivermen.

His ministry at the Mariners' Church continued until 1845, and was notable for his wholehearted, courageous and effective campaign against crimping, his attacks on the vices common on the shipping scene of his day (prostitution, drunkenness, the use of foul language and Sabbath breaking), the influence he had on both sides of the Atlantic in the many areas of maritime ministry in which he was deeply involved, and for sharp disagreements and public controversies with other Christians and Christian organisations engaged in ministry to seafarers. He was also imprisoned for debt on several occasions, though this seems to have been brought about more by his chronic inability to keep proper accounts and the strong antipathies his forceful and determined character occasionally aroused than by dishonesty. The enthusiasm and vision of this extraordinary man seem sometimes to have exceeded the bounds of reasonable caution, but there can be no doubting the extent of his achievements. An eminent contemporary seamen's chaplain in New York, Charles Jones, wrote of him: 'I connect with the name of Smith the commencement of one of the greatest moral revolutions England ever saw; he was the morning star of the sailor's reformation'.[13] Roald Kverndal describes him as 'the Founding Father of organised Christian mission to seamen'.[14]

It is right and proper to pay due tribute to George Smith's role in the development of maritime ministry in the first half of the nineteenth century, but it is equally important to recognise the fact that a great many other fine Christians made leading creative, visionary, enthusiastic and indispensable contributions in many areas of the same field at the same time. In a chapter which is concerned more to sketch a broad picture of the growth and development of the Church's ministry to seafarers than to present a detailed account of its every stage it is impossible to refer by name to many of these wonderful people. It is equally impossible not to write about Smith because of his intimate and vital involvement in much of this pioneering work.

The 1820's saw exciting outreach in a number of directions in Britain. The Bethel movement blossomed in ports around the coast and then spread to every continent. Floating chapels were established at Greenock, Leith, Bristol, Liverpool and Hull. The 'Seamen's Hospital Society for the Relief of Sick and Diseased Seamen arriving in the Port of London' was established on the former H.M.S. 'Grampus', and a decade later on the 'Dreadnought'. A Church of England priest was appointed as chaplain. The Anglican Church established floating churches in Dublin, Liverpool and London, a ship visiting ministry on the Thames, and a shore-based Mariners' Church in Hull. A 'Merchant Seamen's Orphan Asylum' was set up. The 'Royal National Institution for the preservation of Life from Shipwreck' (the forerunner of the present day Royal National Lifeboat Institution) was founded. The 'Shipwrecked and Distressed Sailors' Family Fund' (the forerunner of the present day Shipwrecked Fishermen and Mariners' Royal Benevolent Society) was established. Properly run seamen's lodging houses, whose aim was to protect seamen from the attention of the crimps, were organised by Christian societies in a number of ports, and in London the world's first 'Sailors' Home' was established through the initiative of George Smith.[15]

The imaginative, enthusiastic and far-reaching initiatives of the first thirty years of the nineteenth century were expanded, consolidated and strengthened in the next thirty years, though not without occasional sharp controversy and strife. The Bethel movement flourished in many ports of the world. The British and Foreign Sailors' Society, which was founded in 1833 through the amalgamation of a number of Societies, grew and expanded in influence. It was blessed with wise and visionary guidance from fine Christians like George Angas, a merchant, shipowner, campaigner for the emancipation of slaves, and outstanding pioneer of colonisation in South Australia and New Zealand. In 1856 it opened the innovative and superbly equipped London 'Sailors' Institute', which had a spacious lecture hall, library, reading room, refreshment room with temperance bar, seamen's savings bank, and class rooms for day and nautical schools. In 1835 The Revd. Dr. John Ashley, a young Anglican priest, became aware of the spiritual and physical needs of seamen on board ships in the Bristol Channel. With the backing of the Archbishop of Canterbury he commenced his ministry to seafarers in the Bristol Channel from a small cutter, the 'Eirene'. For fifteen years he visited the ships in all weathers, and he became a trusted and much loved friend and pastor to thousands of seafarers. His work attracted support at the highest level in the Church of England and the maritime world, and as a result of it The Missions to Seamen was founded in 1856. Its aim was to promote the spiritual welfare of seafarers at home and abroad, ashore and afloat. It has become the Anglican Church's worldwide outreach to the seafarers of the world. Also in the 1830's Anglican chaplaincies to seafarers were established in Calcutta and Bombay.

In the United States of America, maritime ministry developed on much the same lines, 'simultaneously and without concert',[16] as in Britain.

In 1812—with Britain and the United States on the brink of war, American merchant shipping tonnage increasing rapidly, and Boston being 'the major port city of the largest ship-owning State in the Union'[17]—a Congregational pastor with Unitarian leanings, Joseph Tuckerman, took the initiative to found the 'Boston Society for the Religious and Moral Improvement of Seamen'. It aimed to distribute 'tracts of a religious and moral nature for the use of seamen', establish 'a

regular divine service on board of our merchant vessels', open
'a school for the instruction of lads at sea', and 'promote
whatever can contribute to the advancement of the best interests of seamen'.[18] Shortly after its foundation the United
States declared war on Britain. The British Navy set up an
effective blockade of the ports on the Eastern seaboard, with
the result that a considerable number of ships lay idle in Boston
and many seamen were unemployed. Inevitably the new Society struggled, and in 1817 it published its last tract. The
concept was superb, but the timing turned out to be disastrous.

An altogether more successful venture took place soon
afterwards in New York. The moving spirit behind it was a
Presbyterian minister, The Revd. Ward Stafford, who in the
religious revival which followed the end of the war with
Britain (late in 1814) was involved in a ministry to the poor
and underprivileged in New York. He discovered the conditions in which seamen lived and worked, noted that many of
them had no permanent home, and observed that they were
'deplorably destitute of religious instruction'.[19] In 1817 he put
forward suggestions as to how this last situation might be
remedied—marine schools could be set up to provide
elementary and navigational instruction in port, Bible
Societies for seamen could be established, and seamen's
churches designed expressly for their use could be built in all
large seaports.[20] He went on to pinpoint the seaman's sense
of separation and isolation from the shoreside community and
his rejection by it. After careful and enthusiastic preparation
'The Society for Promoting the Gospel among Seamen in the
Port of New York' was launched in 1818. Its Board of
Directors represented a number of major denominations, and
Stafford was appointed as pastor and preacher for seamen.

The path of the new Society was by no means smooth, but
Stafford was a man of great determination as well as vision. He
hired a large hall where he held regular well-attended services
for seamen until 1820, when the New York Mariners' Church
was opened. The dedication was performed by ministers of
several Protestant denominations, and the Church could
accommodate up to a thousand people; it had a lecture room
in the basement. With the new Church open and operating
Stafford moved on to new work. He had piloted the building
scheme to completion and arranged the bi-monthly publica-

tion of a seamen's magazine as part of 'The Christian Herald and Seamen's Magazine'. A year after his departure another Presbyterian minister, The Revd. John Truair, was appointed as pastor and fund-raiser for The Mariners' Church, and he too made an enormous impact on maritime ministry in North America.

In the United States, as in Britain, the 1820's was a time of exciting outreach in maritime ministry. The Bethel movement spread to North America and grew rapidly. Fine pastors, such as William Jenks in Boston and Joseph Eastburn in Philadelphia, pioneered and developed ministries among seamen in a number of ports, including Baltimore, Portland (Maine), New Orleans and Savannah. Marine Bible Societies were established, Mariners' Churches were built, and good Christian literature for seamen was prepared and published.

During the 1820's it became clear to John Truair that in addition to the local ministries there was a need for a national organisation to spearhead maritime ministry if it was to make a real impact at every level of American society. His great determination, an excellent public relations campaign, and thorough preparation, led to the foundation in 1826 of the 'American Seamen's Friend Society', whose stated aim was to work on a nationwide basis.

> 'The object of this Society shall be to ameliorate the con-
> dition, and improve the moral and religious character of
> seamen, by the establishment of well-regulated boarding-
> houses, and suitable libraries and reading rooms, when
> practicable; Savings Banks, Register offices, Schools of
> elementary and nautical instruction, by the employment of
> agents for carrying into effect the operation of the Society in
> different parts of the United States, and by the use of such
> other means as may seem calculated to promote the designs
> of the Institution.'[21]

The establishment of the Society was followed by two years of embarrassing lack of activity, but then it forged ahead.

The American Seamen's Friend Society had a great influence on the development of world-wide maritime ministry. At the time of its foundation the American merchant fleet was flourishing. Its ships were trading to many parts of the world and there were many ports where there were American seamen. In 1829 the Society recognised the need to provide a ministry to American seamen in foreign ports, and realised that in so doing there would be a wonderful opportunity to preach the Gospel in non-Christian countries. In 1830 a full-time missionary was sent to Canton in China, and in the next twenty years the Society was represented on a full-time or part-time basis in a number of ports overseas, including Le Havre, Marseilles, Rio de Janeiro, Calcutta, Singapore, Sydney, Cape Town, Cronstadt in Russia, Havana and Honolulu. The foundations of organised maritime ministry on a world scale had been laid, and the scope of the Society's activities expanded steadily.

On the specifically denominational front the Anglican Bishop of Quebec consecrated St. Paul's Chapel for the use of seamen in 1834. In the same year the first steps were taken to launch a comprehensive Episcopalian ministry to seamen in New York, and in 1842 an Episcopal 'Seamen's Mission' was established. In 1844 the Bishop of New York consecrated the 'Floating Church of Our Saviour', and in 1852 a 'missionary at large' was appointed to undertake a waterside ministry. In the 1840's Episcopalian ministries to seafarers were established in Philadelphia, Boston and New Orleans, and in the 1850's in Charleston (South Carolina).

In the United States of America, as in Britain, crimping was a real problem, and the American Seamen's Friend Society made a concerted attack on it by sponsoring boarding houses for seamen and establishing Seamen's Registers to help them obtain employment without the 'assistance' of the landsharks. And, as in Britain, a number of Societies were founded to help sick seamen, and the families of seamen lost at sea.

It was in Britain and the United States of America that organised missions to seamen began.

1860–1914

'The rough islanders treated us with uncommon kindness; because it was cold and had started to rain they lit a bonfire and made us all welcome.'

Acts of the Apostles, chapter 28, verse 2.

On the world scene this was the great age of the British Empire. The Crimean War of 1854-1856 was over, the Indian Mutiny had been put down, the Royal Navy held sway on the oceans, and British trade, territorial possessions and influence were great. In the United States of America the end of the Civil War in 1865 heralded a period of rapid growth in industrialisation, wealth, education and population—from 38 million in 1870 to 92 million in 1910. Slavery was finally abolished. In the Far East Japan opened its doors again to the world after two centuries of self-imposed isolation, the Emperor was restored to the throne, and China and Russia were defeated in war in 1895 and 1904 respectively. Europe, with the exception of the Franco-Prussian War in 1870, was peaceful, but in Africa the Boer War of 1899–1902 was the culmination of years of unrest.

On the Church scene a spirit of questioning was evident in the Reformed Churches. There was indignation and controversy after the publication of Charles Darwin's 'The Origin of the Species' in 1859 and 'The Descent of Man' in 1871. Maintaining that species of living beings evolve by natural selection, the fittest for their biological purpose in each generation alone surviving, Darwin challenged long-cherished and uncritically-held beliefs. In 1860 seven authors, including Frederick Temple (who later became Archbishop of Canterbury), published a collection of articles entitled 'Essays and Reviews', advocating the necessity of free inquiry in religious matters. The book was officially condemned by the Bishops of the Church of England, but interest in it and consideration of the views put forward in it continued. The Christian Socialism propounded by F. D. Maurice, Charles Kingsley and others led many Christians to consider the implications of the Industrial Revolution in a new light, and in 1896 Pope Leo XIII issued the encyclical 'Apostolicae Curae' in which Anglican Orders were condemned as invalid 'through defect of both form and intention'.

On the shipping scene the beginning of this period marks the time when the iron-hulled steam-propelled ship began seriously to undermine the supremacy of the wooden-hulled sailing ship in most areas of marine trading. It must be said at once, however, that sailing ships continued to operate in large

though ever decreasing numbers in some trades until long after
the end of this period.

The first ship in the world to use steam power commercially
was the wooden-hulled stern paddle 'Charlotte Dundas'. She
made her first voyage in 1802 on the Forth and Clyde Canal
towing two lighters. In 1819 the 'Savannah', a United States-
registered sailing ship with an auxiliary engine and detachable
paddles, crossed the Atlantic in twenty-one days. It was
claimed that she was the first steamship to make the crossing,
but apparently she spent only eight hours under steam power
throughout the voyage! In 1837 the Peninsular Steam Navigation Company (later to become the Peninsular and Oriental
Steam Navigation Company and ultimately P. & O.) adver-
tised a fleet of seven steamships. These were ships designed and
built for engines with auxiliary sail power as opposed to ships
built for sail with auxiliary engines.[22] This type of ship continued until the end of the period, by which time far-reaching
improvements had been made in the design and performance
of steam engines, coal consumption had been reduced, iron
hulls had become the norm, screw propellers had replaced
paddles, and ships had got bigger. Significant stages in the
development of steamships were marked by Isambard Kingdom Brunel's three great British-built ships. The 'Great Western', launched in 1838, was a wooden-hulled paddle-steamer
larger than any other steamer of its day. The 'Great Britain',
launched in 1843, was the world's first large iron-hulled
steamship, and the first to be driven by a screw propeller. The
'Great Eastern', which came into service in 1858, was an
enormous iron-hulled vessel of 18,915 tons displacement
driven by paddles and screw propellers and capable of carrying
sufficient coal to take her to and from Australia without
refuelling. She was also the first 'double bottomed ship'.[23]

The introduction of steam propulsion was fiercely resisted in
some quarters, and there were a number of reasons for this.
Steamships were very expensive to build and operate: they
required a full complement of sailing hands as well as engineers, they needed regular supplies of coal for refuelling, and
they had to follow set routes along which they could be assured
of supplies of coal. On the other hand the wind needed to
propel a sailing ship cost nothing. It has also to be said that
many people are resistant to change of any kind at any time,

and indeed in 1828 no less a personage than the First Lord of the Admiralty spelled this out in no uncertain terms. 'Their Lordships feel it their bounden duty,' he said, 'to discourage to the utmost of their ability the employment of steam vessels, as they consider the introduction of steam is calculated to strike a fatal blow at the supremacy of the Empire.'[24]

Despite the determination of the opposition, however, the ultimate supremacy of the steamship over the sailing ship as a fast, reliable and more sophisticated carrier of passengers and cargo in most trades was inevitable. In Britain in the 1830's shipyards were equipping themselves to build steam engines, and the age of the iron-hulled ship was fast approaching. By 1869, the year in which the Suez Canal opened, the tonnage of steamships leaving British shipyards was five times greater than that of sailing vessels,[25] and by 1880 the proportion of steam tonnage under the British flag, which represented 58% of the world's shipping,[26] was two and a half times greater than sailing tonnage. In 1870 William Froude's experiments with model ships in tanks of water introduced a new awareness of the potential of scientific research applied to ship design and construction. Fundamental changes were taking place.

This was the situation in which the churches were ministering to seafarers in the years between 1860 and 1914. It was a period of steady growth, development and expansion of this ministry.

The seaman's life on board began to change with the introduction of iron-hulled steam ships and the recruitment and training of engineers and stokers to man them, but it has to be remembered that it was not until the beginning of the Second World War in 1939 that the sailing ship effectively ceased to be an economically viable form of cargo transport in all but a handful of trades and places. The change was slow. A contemporary description of the crew quarters of one of the best clipper sailing ships of the day by Stanley Treanor, a chaplain of The Missions to Seamen, illustrates this clearly.

'The great roomy space of the forecastle is of the shape of the bows of a ship, narrower at one end than the other, and is lined on both sides with bunks for the crew. There is no table, and underneath the bunks are the seamen's chests,

curious structures, broader at bottom than at top, and
ornamented, all bound with a fringe of plaited rope yarns
. . . In the middle stands a stove, on either side of which run
the great chain cables, out to the anchors through the
hawse-pipes, in which the cables jerk and strain as the ship
rides. The men take their dinner seated on their chests as
before described . . .'[27]

The dangers involved in life at sea at this time were horrific.
In his book 'Flying Angel' L. A. G. Strong records that 'in 1881
more than a thousand British-owned vessels were wrecked,
more than eight hundred of them near the British coast'.[28]
Stanley Treanor[29] vividly describes meetings with seamen on
board ships which foundered at sea only a few days later.

Ashore the seaman's life changed slowly too. It was not until
the beginning of the twentieth century that crimping was
finally stamped out, and the Churches had to tackle realistically and on a worldwide basis the task of providing attractive
and wholesome alternatives to the dockside tavern, gin palace
and brothel as well as countering the activities of the crimps.

During this period the undenominational British and
Foreign Sailors' Society (which became the British Sailors
Society in 1925) and the Anglican Church's organisation The
Missions to Seamen expanded their activities significantly.
Both recognised that the spiritual welfare of seamen would
best be served by a ministry to the whole man—body, mind
and spirit. They saw the need to provide a ship visiting ministry
to the seaman on board his ship, accommodation ashore for
residential, recreational and spiritual purposes, and to fight the
activities of the crimps. In 1860 neither organisation had
significant work outside Britain, but by 1914 the position had
changed greatly. In 1906 The Missions to Seamen was running
62 stations in Britain and 24 overseas, and in 1909 the British
and Foreign Sailors' Society had 28 stations in Britain and 31
overseas.

There were many similarities in the work carried out by the
two organisations. Both ministered to all seafarers—naval
personnel, merchant seamen, fishermen, lighthouse and light-
ship crews—and both carried out shipboard ministries from
sailing boats or steam cutters. They conducted services on
board, provided Bibles, religious tracts and good quality

books and magazines, and gave pastoral help and advice. Stanley Treanor's description of preparing his boat for ship visiting reveals the sort of work they were doing:

'Boxes are got on board the boat containing Bibles and tracts in twenty languages, and the Prayer Book in about ten. Watertight canvas bags containing many volumes of useful and interesting books, and nice bags in which to hang them in the forecastle or cabins of the vessels, are put on board. Another canvas bag, watertight, containing parcels of interesting matter—tracts, magazines, "Illustrated London News", "Graphics", almanacs, besides fifty or a hundred hymn books for the day's work; and another little box containing our temperance pledge-cards, medals and literature. Bags to hold books for sailors, mufflers and mittens . . . needle cases and helmets . . . all made by skilful and loving hands of many ladies . . . also form part of our cargo.'[30]

The ministry provided was pastoral, evangelistic and intensely practical, as the description of a visit by a chaplain to the captain of a large sailing ship reveals:

'He was in deep depression. Having recently come home from a long voyage he found his delicate wife dead; his house empty and closed, and his children scattered in the keeping of various kind friends. He told me of his long efforts to save his wife's life by bringing her to reside in different parts of the world, and of the blow he had received by his bereavement being suddenly made known to him as he returned home full of hope. Tears rolled down his face; no words can describe his thankfulness for sympathy and for prayer, for pray we did to our common Father in the sorrowing captain's inner cabin . . . My poor forlorn brother with me approached the Throne of Grace: human sympathy of other kind was no doubt balm to his torn spirit, but this fellowship in prayer . . . was exactly the fulfilment of his soul's deepest cravings . . .'[31]

Ashore both organisations initially provided reading rooms, chapels and very basic institutes—some of them afloat. In Cardiff, for example, The Missions to Seamen operated from the former H.M.S. 'Thisbe': it was equipped with a Reading Room, had books available to borrow, and games facilities. It also had a chapel which was very well attended: in 1880 no fewer than 25,000 seamen attended Sunday Mattins throughout the year, and 6000 attended the regular mid-week service. Basic though the facilities were, they met a real need and were well used.

The chaplains and port missionaries were men of courage, vision, determination and love. They fought—sometimes literally!—for the seamen. L. A. G. Strong describes the work of The Revd. Arthur Goldsmith in Hong Kong in the late 1880's:

> 'Kowloon, on the mainland opposite Hong Kong, was then a shanty town, with as fine a variety of grog shops and infamous hotels on the waterfront as any other port in the world. Such names as "The Flag of all Nations" and "The Grand" give an idea of the trade their proprietors aimed at . . . Goldsmith started single-handed. He was not robust, but he sometimes had to use his fists to rescue apprentices from the men who had offered to entertain them; and he made strenuous efforts, strongly supported at home, to end the practice of making Sunday a normal working day.'[32]

As the years passed both organisations improved the quality, variety and scope of the facilities they offered to the seamen, and when the British and Foreign Sailors' Society opened 'Jack's Palace' in London in 1903 'its facilities were in their day a wonder to behold . . . there were reading rooms, a restaurant . . . decent private accommodation for seafarers . . . games rooms; a separate wing was provided for foreign seamen, especially of Danish, German and Scandinavian nationality.'[33] It also included the King Edward Nautical School for British and colonial-born sailors.

The two organisations, displaying many similarities in the practical outworking of their ministries, nevertheless differed in some of their emphases. The British and Foreign Sailors' Society carried on the great Bethel tradition and worked with the American Seamen's Friend Society and the newly-established Lutheran Seamen's missions in Scandinavia and

Germany. It was undenominational in structure, looked to all the Reformed Churches for support, and laid great emphasis on its library service. Like The Missions to Seamen it offered its ministry to all seafarers regardless of any considerations of race, rank, religion or ideology. The Missions to Seamen was, and is today, a voluntary international organisation of the Anglican Church working within that Church's structures. Its chaplains were, and are, licensed by their diocesan Bishops, who maintained a keen interest in the work and encouraged support for it. Yet despite their common purpose and the similarities of their ministries there was little contact at any level between the personnel of the two organisations. This sad situation was typical of the attitudes prevailing in the Churches at that time, and the gathering of 1200 delegates from 160 Missionary Boards and Societies at the Edinburgh Missionary Conference in 1910, which resulted in much greater co-operation between the missionary societies and paved the way for inter-confessional collaboration, was a most welcome first step to improve the position.

The early part of this period saw the establishment of the Nordic seamen's missions, and it is important to understand their background in order to appreciate their aims, their way of working, and the contribution they have made to the overall pattern of the Church's ministry to seafarers.

In Scandinavian countries, where the sea has always been a major factor in the lives of the people and the seafarer has traditionally enjoyed a higher social status than in many countries, the Lutheran national Churches were slow to recognise the need for a specific ministry to seafarers. But in the middle of the nineteenth century change was in the air. There was a revival of religion, foreign and home missions were being established, information about the emerging seamen's mission agencies in Britain and the United States of America was being received from Scandinavian seamen, and a number of dynamic pastors recognised the need for a ministry to Scandinavian seamen and pressed ahead to set it up.

In 1860 the British and Foreign Sailors' Society appointed The Revd. August Thiemann as a 'Thames Missionary' with responsibility for foreign, and particularly Scandinavian, seamen. He went to Norway to improve his command of the language and enthusiastically extolled the work of his organisation. He gathered influential support, and in 1861 'The Society for Promoting Religion and Knowledge among Seamen' (Selskabet til befordring af Religiösitet og Kundskab blandt Söfolk) was founded in Stavanger. In Bergen he met The Revd. Johan Storjohan and impressed him deeply with his accounts of the harshness of the seaman's life. In 1863 Storjohan, who was researching in Scotland, preached a sermon to some Scandinavian seamen in Leith. On the following day he was contacted by the mate of a Norwegian ship who had been present and who was in need of pastoral counsel. The incident made a great impact on him, prompting him to say, 'Our seamen must have their own pastors!'[34]

In 1864, and after some initial difficulties, Storjohan and a group of clergymen, merchants and seafarers founded 'The Society for the Proclamation of the Gospel to Scandinavian Seamen in Foreign Ports',[35] which later became 'The Norwegian Seamen's Mission'. It was supported financially by a national network of auxiliaries, voluntary contributions from seamen and shipowners, and by 1914 it had 35 overseas stations. The Norwegian Seamen's Mission has always seen itself as 'the extended arm of the Church of Norway', and its staff are bound by the doctrine, laws and liturgy of the national Church.[36] Its ministry is largely confined to Scandinavians.

Within a decade of the establishment of the Norwegian Seamen's Mission, Denmark (in 1867), Sweden (in 1869), and Finland (in 1875) had set up their own national seamen's mission organisations, and in all of them Storjohan played an important role. Each of these national organisations ministers to its own nationals and to other Scandinavians where their own countries are not represented, and each spread quickly round the world. In 1885 the German Seamen's Mission was established; it too had close ties with the national Lutheran Church.

In 1881 one particular section of the seafaring community —the people who man the deep sea fishing vessels—attracted the attention of a man serving with the Thames Church Mission in London, Ebenezer Mather. In the course of his ministry along a 76 mile stretch of the River Thames, including the whole of the port of London, he had come into contact with many thousands of seamen, bargees, dockers, ships' agents, ships' chandlers and the many others whose business lies in dockland, but had never made a sea voyage himself. A friend challenged him to make a trip on a deep sea trawler out into the North Sea to see for himself the tough conditions in which trawlermen worked. The five day voyage on the 'Supply' changed the direction of his ministry and led to the establishment of the Mission to Deep Sea Fishermen in the same year.

He saw at first hand the heaviness of the work, the physical exposure of the trawlermen to the roughest weather, the lack of proper medical attention for the multitude of injuries which occurred, and the loneliness which is part of the life of every seafarer. A meeting at his home soon afterwards with a trawler captain, whom he had met during his trip and who had subsequently been injured in an accident at sea, led him to press for the provision of a small vessel to provide practical, pastoral, medical and spiritual care for the fishermen. A friend donated a large sum of money, and a 56 ton smack was purchased and re-fitted. Re-named the 'Ensign', she was the first of a series of Mission ships, and soon came to be known as the 'Bethel Ship'. On the day she sailed Thomas Gray, the Chief Executive of the Board of Trade in London, wrote to Mather commending the work and spelling out much of what the young Mission stood for. He wrote:

'There will be many to speak of the spiritual side of your work, and that is important and right, but I want . . . to praise the work-a-day useful work of your Mission in its bearing on the physical and social wellbeing of fishermen. There are people who will not take an interest in matters that are solely religious but who will take a deep and abiding interest in all that concerns the welfare of others . . . Let them think of what you are proposing to do for the fishermen, and so for their families. You propose to give surgical and medical aid to the wounded and sick; you propose to distribute healthy literature to minds that would otherwise be unemployed for long stretches of time; you propose to bring the cheerful influence of home to the crews of the trawlers by the presence among them of this and future Mission smacks; you propose to keep men away from the floating grog ships . . . and as a result you will bring a new safety to property and to limb . . . May you be richly blessed.'[37]

The Mission rapidly made a deep and lasting impact on the fishermen and the fishing communities around the coasts of Britain, and even for a while in Labrador. It lived up to its aim of providing Mission vessels at sea which dispensed medical attention, books, clothes and Christian literature, organised services on board on request, and finally helped to put the floating 'grog' ships out of business. It provided centres for worship and recreation ashore, and a pastoral and evangelistic ministry in the ports where it worked. It still does.

By 1914 it had 11 shore Institutes, 4 sailing smacks and 3 steam powered hospital ships.

The final paragraph in this section deals with the Roman Catholic Church. It is true to say that, while seamen's mission agencies developed and spread around the world in the Reformed Churches throughout the nineteenth century, it was not until the end of the First World War that the Roman Catholic Church really established its particular ministry to seafarers. In the second half of the nineteenth century, however, the beginnings of organised Catholic ministry to seafarers can be discerned. The first Roman Catholic chaplain was appointed to serve with the Royal Navy. French and Dutch priests were ministering to fishermen in Iceland, the Orkneys and Shetland. Concerned priests were forcefully advocating the need for Catholic action on behalf of Catholic seamen. Ship visiting ministries were set up. Seafarers' centres were opened in Bootle, Devonport, Hong Kong, Malta and New York, and an Apostleship of Prayer was organised. The way was being prepared for the foundation of the Apostleship of the Sea in 1921.

Notes

1. Archdeacon John Owen, Chaplain General of the Royal Navy, 1811.
2. Boswell's 'Life of Johnson', March 1759.
3. Roald Kverndal, 'Seamen's Missions, Their Origin and Early Growth' 1987, p. 53.

4. Ibid. p. 54.

5. Ibid. p. 53.

6. Ibid. p. 52.

7. 'In the early nineteenth century insanity in the Royal Navy was seven times the national average. The distinguished surgeon Sir Gilbert Blane (1749–1834) . . . suggested that this was due to head injuries caused by men constantly bumping their heads in the confined spaces between decks, which they naturally did more frequently when drunk!' Guinness Book of Ships and Shipping 1983.

8. Kverndal, 'Seamen's Missions, Their Origin and Early Growth', p. 328.

9. Ibid. p. 58.

10. Ibid. p. 71.

11. Ibid. p. 184.

12. Ibid. p. 268.

13. Ibid. p. 362.

14. Ibid. p. 364.

15. Ibid. p. 424.

16. Ibid. p. 407.

17. Ibid. p. 409.

18. Ibid. p. 419.

19. Ibid. p. 419.

20. Ibid. p. 457.

21. Ibid. p. 457.

22. 'The Story of P. & O.' by David and Stephen Howarth 1987, p. 13.

23. The double bottom is the space between the outer skin on the bottom of a ship and the watertight plating over the floors. It has two purposes: it is a protection against disaster when the outer bottom is holed, and it provides convenient stowage for liquid ballast. See Oxford Companion to Ships and the Sea, p. 261.

24. Quoted by David and Stephen Howarth 'The Story of P. & O.' 1987, p. 15.

25. L. A. G. Strong 'Flying Angel' 1956, p. 4.

26. The Revd. David Harries, Superintendent Chaplain, British Sailors' Society, 1988.

27. 'The Log of a Sky Pilot', by The Revd. Stanley Treanor, a chaplain of The Missions to Seamen, published in 1893, p. 60.

28. 'Flying Angel' by L. A. G. Strong 1956, p. 50.

29. See note 27.

30. 'The Log of a Sky Pilot'. S. Treanor 1893, pp. 31, 32.

31. Ibid. pp. 40, 41.

32. L. A. G. Strong, 'Flying Angel' 1956, pp. 53, 54.

33. The Revd. David Harries, Superintendent Chaplain, British Sailors Society.

34. Kverndal, 'Seamen's Missions, Their Origin and Early Growth' p. 600.

35. Ibid. p. 601.

36. Ibid. p. 602.

37. 'Fish and Ships' Stanley Pritchard, 1980, pp. 21, 22.

III The Development of Maritime Ministry in the 20th Century

1914–1960

'We found out when the war was on what we owed to sailors.'—The Bishop of London at the Annual General Meeting of The Missions to Seamen in 1921.

The years between 1914 and 1960 were a time of political and social upheaval, global warfare, and rapid scientific, technological and medical advance. What happened in all these areas profoundly affected the life, work and witness of the Churches, and their maritime ministry was no exception.

On the world scene four distinct revolutions swept through Europe in the first half of the twentieth century. The democratic revolution saw universal suffrage become the norm in many countries, while the Communist revolution in Russia, the Fascist revolution in Italy, and the Nazi revolution in Germany all influenced the political, social and ideological outlook of people throughout the world. The world wars of 1914–18 and 1939–45 involved most of the developed nations, and the numbers of people killed or injured were astronomical. The dropping of the atomic bombs on Hiroshima and Nagasaki introduced a chilling new element into warfare.

On the scientific and technological front there was far-reaching progress. The invention of the internal combustion engine at the end of the nineteenth century and its subsequent development, the introduction of radio and later of television, the ever-increasing sophistication of inter-personal communications, the splitting of the atom and the application of nuclear power to everyday life, the phenomenal development of the aeroplane, the wide-ranging advances in medicine and surgery, and the entry of man into space, all brought irreversible change to the lives of most people.

On the Church scene the Edinburgh Missionary Conference of 1910 had pointed the Reformed Churches towards the path of growing understanding, increasing collaboration and greater unity. The 1920 Lambeth Conference of Anglican Bishops reflected this new attitude when it said that, 'We do not ask that any one communion should consent to be absorbed in another. We do ask that all should unite in a new and great endeavour to recover and to manifest to the world the unity of the Body of Christ for which He prayed.'[1]

However progress was anything but rapid. Firmly-held beliefs and basic attitudes respond slowly to fresh thinking. Much groundwork had to be done before real progress could be made. But the inauguration in 1947 of the Church of South India, which brought together in one Church Anglicans, Congregationalists, Methodists and Presbyterians, marked a significant step forward in ecumenism, and right at the end of the period the historic papacy of John XXIII opened doors towards unity which many had thought were permanently closed.

In the maritime world change was rapid and comprehensive. The development of the diesel engine, and its application to ships just before the First World War, brought about another revolution in ship propulsion and design. It also initiated a new trade, since oil had to be transported from where it was to where it was needed. In 1912 the British Navy made the decision to change from coal to diesel fuel, and most modern navies quickly followed suit, though naturally it took time for the changeover to be completed. Also in 1912 the first merchant ship to be classified as a motor ship, the 1179 ton 'Vulcanus' built in Amsterdam, was registered at Lloyds.

The period between the two World Wars was the golden age of the passenger liner. Fine ships like P & O's 'Viceroy of India' (built in 1929), Cunard's 'Queen Mary' (launched in 1934) and 'Queen Elizabeth' (launched in 1938), and the French 'Normandie', provided fast, comfortable, regular and reliable service. In 1937 the 'Queen Mary' and the 'Normandie' vied regularly for the notional Blue Riband award for the fastest crossing of the Atlantic, and their average speed of around 30 knots was only surpassed by the 'United States' in 1952. It was also the age of the oil tanker. A large number of tankers of around 12,000 deadweight tons (d.w.t.) were built

Stef Courtlee   p 130

1972-75

2nd Play Demmle's
General Rec — Tom terpot
(6y) Applied — From 1 senetate
     Penna '8 Four Inylish) 13/
     Bio Papers..

then, their size being limited by the capacity of the Suez Canal, and it was not until after the Second World War that a number of new factors brought about a tremendous growth in their size and capacity. By 1960 the largest tanker afloat was more than 100,000 d.w.t.

The Second World War saw the introduction of a number of specially designed ships, like tank landing craft and the landing ship dock, and the technology involved in designing and building them and other innovative vessels was later adapted, developed and incorporated in the present day Roll on/Roll off (Ro-Ro), Lighter Aboard Ship (L.A.S.H.) and container ships. Throughout the period ship design and construction developed steadily and at times rapidly, cargo handling methods improved slowly, and ships became safer. By the end of the period, though, the aeroplane had taken over much of the passenger carrying trade, and the day of the passenger liner was almost over, even though the year 1960 saw the launching or entry into service of such great ships as 'Orlanza' for Royal Mail, 'Empress of Canada' for Canadian Pacific, 'Leonardo da Vinci' for the Italia Line, 'Windsor Castle' for Union Castle, 'Canberra' for P & O and the 'United States' and 'France'.[2] Shipping companies diversified their interests.

This was the background against which the churches were ministering to seafarers between 1914 and 1960, and just as the changes were rapid and far-reaching in most areas of life so in this particular ministry the Churches moved swiftly and effectively to keep pace with what was happening.

The two organisations ministering to seafarers of all nationalities which at the beginning of this period were already established on a limited worldwide basis, the British and Foreign Sailors' Society and The Missions to Seamen, found themselves faced with enormous challenges at the beginning of the First World War in 1914. The ways in which they developed as a result of these challenges are significant.

In 1914 The British and Foreign Sailors' Society registered its Sailors' Homes in Britain with the Admiralty. Most were used for emergency purposes or temporary hospital accommodation. In 1917 the Society opened an orphanage for children of Royal Navy or Merchant Navy personnel killed in the war. In 1920 it opened the Prince of Wales Sea Training

School at Limehouse in London to train boys for service in the Merchant Navy. In the early 1920's, when a severe recession hit the shipping industry and many seafarers were unemployed, it appointed as its Welfare Superintendent The Revd. George Dempster, a Free Church minister, who graphically and movingly described his work in a series of books, such as 'Touched by a Loving Hand', and 'The Love that will not let me go'. His work led to the establishment of the present 'Personal Affairs Office', which caringly and efficiently handles any sort of pastoral or family problem referred to it by seafarers or shipping companies. It is a service which is much appreciated throughout the shipping industry in Britain and beyond. In 1924 the Society had 46 centres, of which 17 were overseas. In 1925 it changed its name to the 'British Sailors' Society', dropping the word 'Foreign' though continuing to minister to all seafarers. In 1932 almost one and a half million seafarers used its centres, and an indication of the terrible problems caused by the continuing unemployment of seamen is the figure of more than 100,000 free meals served in that year. Between the two world wars the Society opened new centres in a number of ports, including London, Haifa and Southampton.

During the Second World War the Society reacted splendidly to emergency conditions. It provided rescue outfits for survivors of ships sunk at sea, an ambulance launch for use on the Clyde, and New Testaments and books of prayers in every lifeboat on British-registered ships. Its centres operated at full stretch. The Prince of Wales Sea Training School was used by the Admiralty as a centre to train merchant seamen in defensive warfare, and the Society also ran a rest centre for war-weary naval personnel. Its centres in Malta and Hamburg were destroyed.

After the Second World War the Society settled down again to its daily ministry among the seafarers of the world, but in an industry which began to change rapidly.

The Anglican Church's organisation, The Missions to Seamen, began the First World War with 74 stations, (of which 19 were overseas), and ended it with 125, (of which 43 were overseas). By then it had 97 chaplains and 77 Lay Readers.[3] As the Bishop of London said at the Society's Annual General Meeting in 1921, 'We found out when the war was on what we owed to sailors.' Between the wars the Society modernised and re-equipped many of its centres, coped with the appalling hardship and suffering caused to seamen by long term un- employment, replaced some of its centres, and opened a number of new ones, including those at Bunbury, Fremantle, Port Lincoln, Port Pirie, Durban, Mombasa and Glasgow. In 1935 the Society had 96 stations, of which 51 were overseas.

The beginning of the Second World War in 1939 found the Society fully staffed with chaplains and lay readers, and with up-to-date centres. In 1940 all the stations in continental Europe were expropriated, and many in the United Kingdom were badly damaged by bombs. Somehow they all kept going, though the staff and volunteers often worked in conditions of great danger, as an extract from the Tilbury chaplain's report on his launch work makes clear:

'Next day there was a raid much nearer home, and shrapnel fell about us like hail. We arrived back safely only to find trouble waiting for us there. A large ship was on fire. Ammunition was blowing up, and quite a number of British and European sailors were lying about wounded or dead. The Chaplain and his assistant did all they could.'[4]

In Belfast 700 volunteers served a total of four and a half million meals to seafarers in temporary mission premises. On the Tyne the distressing task of constantly breaking news of death to the families of seafarers brought the Chaplain himself to an early grave. Overseas new stations were opened in Halifax (Nova Scotia), Port of Spain (Trinidad) and Freetown (Sierra Leone), and in South Africa the Cape Town and Durban stations did sterling work. Durban was famed for its 'All Night Inn', where a seamen could enjoy a comfortable bed, a bath and a cup of tea at minimal cost. The Chaplains in Hong Kong and Singapore were imprisoned by the Japanese. Both carried out wonderful ministries among their fellow prisoners, and the Singapore chaplain, The Revd. Victor Wardle, died there in 1945 from malaria and malnutrition. In Japan the stations in Kobe and Yokohama carried on their work through local volunteers after the chaplains were withdrawn in 1941.

'Flying Angel* acted as if both bodily and spiritual help were one. In the war many seamen, like thousands in other walks of life, for the first time found their spiritual hunger. Survivors of shipwreck declared that, in an open boat in the Atlantic, they prayed as they had never prayed before; and having by some miracle returned to port, they worshipped in the chapels of the Flying Angel . . . For many, war was a time of spiritual birth or rebirth. Flying Angel did its utmost not to fail a tremendous opportunity.'[5]

After the war the Society reverted to its peace-time role. It recruited Honorary Chaplains to minister to seafarers where there was no full-time representation, and opened new work as opportunities and resources presented themselves. Its centres, like those of the British Sailors' Society, provided excellent recreational facilities, including billiards, darts, table tennis, table games and cinema shows, and also a chapel, shop, canteen, and sometimes residential accommodation. The staff and volunteers, led by the Chaplain, did their best to make each centre a Christian home-away-from-home.

Without doubt, though, the most significant happening in the sphere of maritime ministry in this period was the establishment on a world-wide basis in 1921 of the Roman Catholic Apostleship of the Sea.

It has already been noted that towards the end of the nineteenth century and in the early years of the twentieth a number of Catholic ministries to seafarers had been set up, but Peter Anson, one of the founders of the Apostleship of the Sea, points out that 'between 1900 and 1920 . . . the Catholic Sea Apostolate steadily declined, except in a few ports, such as Montreal and New York. The Brothers of St. Vincent de Paul still carried on ship visiting, (and) in France the Société des Oeuvres de Mer managed to continue its magnificent work among deep sea fishermen.'[6] In 1920 there were 11 Seamen's Institutes, 1 Hostel with sleeping accommodation, no Honorary Port Chaplains, and 13 Organised Committees for ship visiting and other services operating under the auspices of the

---

* The name by which The Missions to Seamen is familiarly known. Its logo is an angel carrying the Gospel to all the peoples of the world and is based on Revelation Chapter 14 verse 6.

Roman Catholic Church. An Apostleship of Prayer continued to function.

The impetus for the establishment of the Apostleship of the Sea came from the Benedictine Community on the island of Caldey off the coast of South Wales. The lives of the monks were closely linked with the sea. They owned several boats, in some of which limestone from the island's quarries was exported, and they were committed to pray daily for those at sea. Their particular concern was the spiritual welfare of Catholic seafarers. In 1917 an Oblate Brother of the Community, Brother Richard,* took over the direction of the Apostleship of Prayer, and he became further involved with ministry to seafarers when a request came from the Admiralty to revise the Lists of Catholic Churches (which gave details of the times of Sunday Masses and the distances of the churches from various landing places). When letters stressing the need for action by the Catholic Church on behalf of Catholic merchant seafarers began to appear in influential Catholic publications, Brother Richard undertook a fact-finding tour of ports in the United Kingdom and Ireland.

He visited the Catholic Seamen's Home in London and was distressed to note 'how badly it compared with the majority of Protestant Homes in London and elsewhere'.[7] However his visit to Glasgow during that tour bore rich fruit.

In the Catholic Press a naval chaplain pointed out that 'unlike the Navy, the men of the Mercantile Marine have no chaplains, and ... priests in seaport towns are too overburdened with work already to be able to give ships much individual attention. Why not a Society of Catholic Chaplains to Merchant Seamen?'[8] In an article in 'The Month' in 1920 the Secretary of the Montreal Catholic Sailors Club, Dr. W. H. Atherton, posed the following questions:

1. What are Catholics doing for the men and women of the Mercantile Marine?
2. How many institutions in the world do Catholics provide for the wandering seafaring class?
3. What can be done at once for them? and
4. How can sailor missions or clubs be financed?

* Brother Richard was Peter Anson's community name. His natural modesty caused him to avoid publicising his own part in the establishment of the Apostleship of the Sea.

He went on to quote a naval chaplain who had written that, 'this work of ministering to merchant seamen cannot be carried out on board until the dream be realised that a priest be stationed in each of the great foreign harbours, and for the work entirely—and it must be done in the home ports'.[9]

In Glasgow the ministry of ship visiting had been revived, and Brother Richard made another visit. In 1921 he wrote that 'some day we hope that all these local efforts may be joined up in one great Society of Catholic Missions to Seamen'[10] and was generous in his acknowledgement of the work already being carried out by both the British and Foreign Sailors' Society and The Missions to Seamen.[11] He tells how the concept of the Apostleship of the Sea was born in his mind during a fishing trip to Scotland:

'We had been fishing all night, and the member of the crew whose turn it was to take his watch, asked me to relieve him, telling me the course to steer. He was soon fast asleep at my feet. The sun rose above the horizon. It was a flat calm, with scarcely a breath of wind; no sound but the steady throb of the engines, and the swish of water beneath the bows, and the harsh scream of gulls. I took out my Benedictine "Horae Diurnae", and with one hand on the wheel, and an occasional peep at the compass, recited the Office of Lauds. As my shipmate slept peacefully and "Morning Star" steamed north east, the whole idea of an international society devoted to the welfare of seafarers fell into shape.'[12]

Shortly afterwards provisional Rules and Constitutions for a new-style Apostleship of the Sea were drawn up and officially recognised by the Catholic hierarchies in England, Scotland, Wales and Ireland. The Rules stated that:

'The Apostleship of the Sea is a Society of Catholic men and women united together in prayer and work for the greater glory of God, and the spiritual welfare of seafarers throughout the world.'[13]

The methods to be employed would be active work—ship visiting in ports, distribution of Catholic literature, the provision of means and places of recreation for Catholic seafarers, keeping Catholic seafarers in touch with the Church and each other by means of an International Sailors League—daily prayer, and receiving Holy Communion at least once a year for the intentions of the Apostleship.[14] There were to be Parochial Committees, Diocesan Councils, and, once the work became firmly established, a Superior Council.

In 1922 Brother Richard, who had spent some time in Belgium and France and found lively interest in maritime ministry there, made a visit to Rome, and submitted the Rules and Constitutions of the Apostleship of the Sea to the Vatican. On April 17th 1922 His Holiness the Pope gave his formal approval, encouragement and blessing to the work.

The growth and expansion of the Apostleship of the Sea was rapid and extraordinary, as a glance at the statistics below reveals:

	1920	1927	1932
Institutes	11	17	40
Hostels (sleeping accommodation)	1	1	6
Hon. Port Chaplains	0	1	14
Organised Committees for ship visiting and other services[15]	13	31	60

In 1930 the congress at Liverpool set up an International Council (Apostolatus Maris Internationale Concilium) whose task was to co-ordinate the efforts of all groups of workers in the Sea Apostolate and provide an international clearing-house for all such groups. It would respect the autonomy of individual Apostolatus Maris groups throughout the world. The broad outlines of the work of the Apostleship of the Sea were defined, and it is clear that the Apostleship of the Sea was pressing ahead rapidly, underpinned by the prayers of the faithful. In 1938 there were 317 ports in the world where merchant seafarers were 'provided with means of contact with the (Catholic) Church'.[16]

The Second World War affected the Apostleship of the Sea in many of the same ways as it did the British Sailors' Society and The Missions to Seamen. Some new apostolates were established, while others had to be temporarily suspended.

The post-war years saw it forge ahead. It gave a lead in the type and quality of facilities and services provided for seafarers in a rapidly changing world, and the magnificently equipped and furnished Stella Maris* Centres in Bootle, Hull and London introduced a new concept of comfort, care and concern for the seafarer.

In North America those involved in maritime ministry were spared some of the traumas of war (bombing, invasion and occupation) which were experienced by their counterparts in Europe and several other parts of the world. The welcome they provided all over the continent for seafarers visiting their ports and centres was unfailingly warm, generous and understanding—and very much appreciated.

In the United States of America ministry to seafarers, with the exception of the Roman Catholic Apostleship of the Sea, developed along the lines of individual legally separate agencies related to, involved with but not dependent on parent Churches or Church organisations. The people engaged in this work have invariably been determined, go-ahead 'self-starters' who worked hard and achieved much. In Canada the Anglican Church's ministry developed in association with The Missions to Seamen, the Roman Catholic Church's through the Apostleship of the Sea, and the British Sailors' Society was also present in a number of ports. In 1932 a great step forward in inter-agency and inter-Church collaboration was taken in North America with the formation of the National Group of Seamen's Agencies. This later became the National (and in 1967 the International) Council of Seamen's Agencies for North America and the Caribbean, and it played a key role in the establishment of the International Christian Maritime Association at Rotterdam in 1969.

The Nordic and German Seamen's Missions, with their Lutheran and national orientation, developed along the lines of providing a pastoral and evangelistic ministry to seafarers of their own countries in overseas ports, and usually within the framework of a local expatriate congregation and church. Their seamen's centres were comfortable, well-equipped Christian homes-away-from-home and were much appreciated by seafarers. Their chaplains and other staff were held in high respect.

* Stella Maris is the name often given to the seafarers' centres of the Apostleship of the Sea.

1960–1985

'In some essentially intuitive way Pope John had decided that the Church needed a change.'

Adrian Hastings[17]

This period in world history is notable for an uneasy peace between the United States of America and the Soviet Union (the world's super-powers), prolonged armed conflicts in Vietnam, Central America, the Middle East, Northern Ireland and Afghanistan, the emergence of China as a world power, increasing hostility to and the isolation of the white government in South Africa, the increasing militancy and rapid growth of Islam, continuing rapid scientific and technological advance, and a growing realisation that 'anything that happens anywhere in the world can produce effects very rapidly elsewhere'.[18]

On the Church scene Pope John XXIII initiated fundamental changes in the life, work and attitudes of the Roman Catholic Church. He called together a world congress of Roman Catholic leaders (the Second Vatican Council), and set it the task of renewing the religious life of the Church and bringing up-to-date its teaching, discipline and organisation. The ultimate goal was the unity of all Christian people. Meeting between 1962 and 1965, in four sessions each lasting between two and three months, the impact of this Council, 'the most important ecclesiastical event of this century, not just for Roman Catholics but for all Christians',[19] was as welcome as it was far-reaching. With it dawned an age of progress in mutual understanding between the Roman Catholic and Reformed Churches, joint discussions on doctrinal issues, common acts of worship, and collaboration at many levels. In the Reformed Churches progress towards unity was being made in many parts of the world, as the inauguration of the Church of North India in 1970 confirmed: this Church brought together Anglicans, the United Church of North India (itself a union of Congregationalists and Presbyterians), Methodists, Baptists, the Church of the Brethren and the Disciples of Christ. There were set-backs, too—the failure in England in 1969 of the Anglican-Methodist reunion scheme 'reduced the Church of England from comprehension to incoherence'[20]—but there can be little doubt that deep down at grass roots level a growing desire for greater unity between the Churches was springing up.

On the shipping scene the introduction of containerisation in the late 1960's revolutionised the whole concept of dry cargo handling, and three closures of the Suez Canal within twenty years from 1956 led to the development of the Very Large (V.L.C.C.) and Ultra Large Crude (oil) Carrier (U.L.C.C.) and the big bulk carrier. A number of new special-ised types of ships, like the motor car carrier, roll on/roll off ships (R.O.R.O.), Lighter Aboard Ship Vessels (L.A.S.H.), Liquid Natural Gas Carriers (L.N.G.) and Oil/Bulk/Ore (O.B.O.) ships, came into service.* The passenger liner, to the sorrow of many, passed into history. The great passenger vessels were switched to pleasure cruising, and passenger ferries became more sophisticated. A crippling worldwide trade recession followed the astronomical rises in the price of oil in 1973, and many long-established shipowners either combined with others to form consortia or drastically reduced the size of their fleets. There was a sharp decline in the number of ships registered in developed countries, and a corresponding increase in the number registered under flags of convenience.† There was also a steep decrease in the number of seafarers from developed countries, and a rapid rise in the number from developing (especially Asian) countries. With the increasing automation of ships, the reduced numbers of seafarers re-quired to man them, the availability of more seafarers for jobs than jobs for seafarers, the over-supply of certain types of ships and razor-sharp competition for trade, a significant number of seafarers experienced unjust treatment in the form of non-payment of wages, being stranded in ports far from home when their companies changed hands or were bankrupted, serving on ships with inadequate safety standards, and being 'blacklisted' if they complained.

This was the setting in which the Churches ministered to seafarers in the years between 1960 and 1985. The political, economic and technological developments throughout the world, the blossoming of the ecumenical movement in the

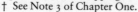

* A more detailed description of these various types of vessels may be found in Chapter Four, 'The Shipping Scene in the late 1980's'.
† See Note 3 of Chapter One.

Churches, and the revolution in merchant shipping combined under the hand of God to bring about a remarkable growing together of the different traditions of ministry in the maritime world in a movement which is still gathering momentum.

The contributions made by the individual denominational and undenominational organisations to the development of maritime ministry have been briefly traced, (though it is a source of regret that considerations of space preclude full coverage of the whole spectrum of Christian service in the seafaring world, which includes provision for retired seafarers, sick seafarers, the families of seafarers who have died at sea, and educational and library facilities, etc., etc.). All brought their separate and individual emphases to the work. They were blessed with many dynamic and visionary chaplains, lay staff, voluntary helpers and supporters. By the end of the period under review they were represented altogether in some nine hundred ports all over the world.

The services they provided for seafarers were impressive and comprehensive. Seafarers were visited on board their ships and in hospitals, training establishments and detention centres in ports all over the world. Centres where seafarers could change their money, do their shopping, telephone home, have a meal or a drink, relax in comfortable surroundings, enjoy a game of snooker or table tennis, watch a film, meet seafarers of other countries, meet local Christian people, attend Christian worship or seek advice or spiritual help, were provided in most of the busy ports outside the Communist bloc countries.* Practical services—like providing transport from the ship to the seafarers' centre and back again (a godsend when the ship is berthed a long way from the centre, time is short and the weather unpleasant), supplying libraries, books, magazines, papers, films and videos, and arranging sightseeing tours and sporting activities—were universal. Representing the interests of seafarers to port officials, union representatives, shipping agents, shipowners and government officials, was all part of the day's work. Above all, these Christian organisations made the Church visible and real to seafarers, proclaiming the Living Jesus by quality of life, the spoken word, actions, making

---

* In some Communist countries, notably the Soviet Union, international seafarers' centres are provided by the government.

Christian literature available, and caring for all without regard
to considerations of race, rank, creed or ideology. In a period
of revolutionary change in the shipping world the Churches
both adapted their work to changed circumstances and provided stability and security for an increasingly anxious and
insecure seafaring community.

In 1969 an historic conference was held in Rotterdam. It
was described as an 'International Consultation on Services to
Seafarers', and the initiative for it came jointly from the
International Council of Seamen's Agencies in North America
and the World Council of Churches. It was jointly sponsored
by the Apostleship of the Sea, the British Sailors' Society, the
International Council of Seamen's agencies, The Missions
to Seamen, the Nederlandse Zeemanscentrale, the Nordic
Missions to Seamen and the World Council of Churches.
Delegates from 52 national and international Christian
voluntary organisations serving among seafarers attended.

The aim of the Consultation was to study and assess contemporary seafaring life, to examine how far its problems and
needs were being met by Christian agencies, to assess what
further provision was required and to agree upon and formulate appropriate action to be taken at local, national and
international level.

As the conference progressed it became apparent to all
present that momentous decisions were going to be taken.
Enthusiasm and excitement took hold of delegates from
widely different traditions, backgrounds and temperaments.
Barriers crumbled and then fell. As one delegate said afterwards, 'The Holy Spirit was at work among us.'[21]

At the end of the Consultation there was unanimous agreement among the Christian voluntary organisations to establish
a voluntary association 'to achieve collaboration in the furtherance of their common aims and to serve as a means to more
effective co-operation with other agencies.'[22] A committee
was set up to study the way in which such a permanent
association, whose nature would be consultative and representative rather than jussive or prescriptive, might be brought
into being. In addition to fostering collaboration and mutual
aid the association would aim to be 'the collective and respected voice'[23] of them all. It would be financed by its
member organisations.

Thus the International Christian Maritime Association (I.C.M.A.) came into being. Immediately after its formation preparations began for its first plenary conference, which was to be held in London in 1972. The conference built on the foundations laid in Rotterdam and was another time of joyful fellowship and goodwill. This and future plenary conferences held regularly every three or four years brought together chaplains, lay staff and voluntary workers of many denominations in a process of getting to know and understand each other better, worshipping together, sharing their hopes and fears, enjoying each other's company, discussing their work and experience, planning joint action and moving towards that unity which our Lord Jesus Christ desires for His Church. Then regular regional conferences were arranged for the years between the plenary ones; they dealt with matters of regional and international importance and, like the plenary conferences, were invaluable in promoting understanding, goodwill and collaboration.

The impact of the International Christian Maritime Association was immediate, and its influence grew steadily. In 1976 The Revd. Prebendary Tom Kerfoot became the first General Secretary, working on a part-time basis. He had been one of the key people in the establishment of the association, had served with The Missions to Seamen (as a chaplain and latterly as General Secretary) for thirty-nine years, and was the ideal person for the task. He worked from an office in the vestry of St. Michael Paternoster Royal, the Central Office of The Missions to Seamen, and he guided the association wisely until his retirement in 1982. He was succeeded by The Revd. Bernard Krug, a Lutheran pastor serving with the German Seamen's Mission in Felixstowe, where he had led an interconfessional chaplaincy team and seen a new seafarers' centre established. Active, enthusiastic, concerned, energetic—and with a delightful sense of humour—he has coaxed, cajoled and sometimes driven the Association forward.

While it is right and proper to say that the birth of the International Christian Maritime Association in 1969 was followed by practical implementation of many of the resolutions on which it was established, and particularly in the sphere of the promotion of interconfessional collaboration, it should also be made clear that before 1969 there was ample evidence of a growing willingness and desire for such collaboration. In North America the annual conference of the International Council of Seamen's Agencies (I.C.O.S.A.), which was established in 1951*, brought together representatives of denominational, undenominational and secular agencies caring for seafarers in North America and the Caribbean. I.C.O.S.A. played a key role in the establishment of the International Christian Maritime Association, recognising the need for such a body to operate on a world-wide basis. In Britain the British Sailors' Society and The Missions to Seamen set up the Seafarers' Trust in the 1960's to be the trustee body for new operations they undertook together. In 1967 a magnificent new seafarers' centre in Fremantle, Western Australia, replaced the two separate centres the Societies had been operating. In 1969 a joint ministry was established in rented premises in the rapidly growing Western Australian port of Port Hedland, and in 1973 the Apostleship of the Sea joined the two Societies in building a splendid new seafarers' centre there. In 1969 the Apostleship of the Sea accepted an invitation from the Anglican Bishop of Hong Kong, the Committee of the Mariners' Club in Hong Kong and The Missions to Seamen, to work in and from the Mariners' Club as partners in ministry. Individual chaplains engaged in maritime ministry in the early and mid 1960's have testified to a spirit of friendliness and willingness to co-operate with each other among the staff of the various organisations. In the writer's own experience at that time it was chaplains of the Apostleship of the Sea, the German Seamen's Mission and the Nordic Seamen's Missions who began his ecumenical education. The way had been prepared for the establishment of the International Christian Maritime Association.

After the International Christian Maritime Association came into being a period of rationalisation of resources in maritime ministry quickly followed in many parts of the world. In every continent there were notable examples of chaplains, lay staff, voluntary workers and committee members, encouraged by their Bishops and ecclesiastical hierarchies, sitting down together to work out how they could make the best use of their individual resources, be partners in ministry, and promote the unity of Christ's Body, the Church.

* See origins of ICOSA on page 50.

In Antwerp, in the early 1970's, the work of the Apostleship of the Sea, the British Sailors' Society, the German Seamen's Mission and The Missions to Seamen was brought together under one roof at the Stella Maris Club of the Apostleship of the Sea, under the wise guidance of the Roman Catholic chaplain, Father Alphonse Laureys. A second centre, to be jointly operated, was built in the container port, and the relationship between the Societies was established on as informal a basis as possible. In Japan in 1975 the Anglican and Roman Catholic Bishops of Kobe publicly and formally signed an agreement for The Missions to Seamen and the Apostleship of the Sea to work together in Kobe from the premises of The Missions to Seamen, which were then re-named The Kobe Mariners' Centre. In Australia the Apostleship of the Sea accepted invitations from The Missions to Seamen to work together in Brisbane and Newcastle from the premises of The Missions to Seamen, and in Adelaide the Apostleship of the Sea and later The Missions to Seamen accepted invitations from the British Sailors' Society to work as partners in ministry from their building. In South America in 1975 The Missions to Seamen accepted an invitation to work as partners in ministry with the Apostleship of the Sea from the Stella Maris Club in Buenos Aires, and in the United States of America a unique ecumenically operated seafarers centre was established in Houston in 1971. There a group of business people combined to build the centre, and they made it available to the Churches on condition that there would be no religious barriers. It is a magnificent centre, well used, well equipped, and very well run by a large inter-confessional chaplaincy team. In Canada, after one abortive attempt, a happy partnership in ministry between The Missions to Seamen, the Apostleship of the Sea and the British Sailors' Society was established in Vancouver, using the premises of The Missions to Seamen. In Africa The Missions to Seamen and the Apostleship of the Sea became partners in ministry in Lagos and Dar es Salaam. In Port Elizabeth in South Africa the Apostleship of the Sea and The Missions to Seamen work in partnership with the Sailors' Society of South Africa, using the Sailors' Society's premises, and in Durban the same three Societies and the German Seamen's Mission work together from an old centre in the city and a fine new one, jointly financed and operated, in the Bay Head area of the port.

In Indonesia in the late 1970's and early 1980's a magnificent seafarers' centre was built in Tanjung Priok, the port of Jakarta, by the German Seamen's Mission in partnership with the Apostleship of the Sea, The Missions to Seamen, the Indonesian Council of Churches and later the British Sailors' Society. The partners experienced incredible frustrations in their dealing with local officialdom but eventually all was happily resolved, and in 1986 they transferred ownership to the Indonesian Communion of Churches. The German Seamen's Mission has promised guidance from a chaplain on the spot for a limited period of time, the partners are giving financial support, and the Church locally is running the operation. These are random examples of the interconfessional collaboration which is a fact in so many ports of the world. A more comprehensive review, analysis and assessment of current interconfessional collaboration may be found in the chapters dealing with the Nature of the Church's Ministry to Seafarers Today and the International Christian Maritime Association.

The spread of interconfessional collaboration in maritime ministry was impressive, but it would be quite untrue to say that everyone involved in this ministry accepted the principle and practice of it joyfully, wholeheartedly or immediately. There were some in every organisation who were hesitant to commit themselves to it, and others who accepted it in principle but found it difficult in practice. Very few were actually opposed to it.[24] As collaboration developed, however, the visible benefits of it became apparent. Seafarers saw that the Churches can and do pray together, plan together and work together. The element of 'competition' between the various seafarers' organisations decreased dramatically. Christians of all denominations were enriched by closer contact with people of other traditions. The pastoral care of seafarers and their families was enhanced. Maritime ministry was recognised by Churches all over the world by the introduction in the mid 1970's of the observance of Sea Sunday on the second Sunday in July. The Churches began to speak with one voice on major issues. Regular inter-confessional meetings took place, and a deepening fellowship and unity of purpose became apparent.

The increasing collaboration of the organisations ministering to seafarers enabled them to present a united front in dealing with the major issues of the maritime scene of the day. Unemployment became an increasingly serious problem for seafarers—it was an almost inevitable result of the combination of containerisation, automation, reduced manning levels, the training of too many seafarers, worldwide trade recession, cut-throat competition for business and 'flagging out'.[25] The numbers of seafarers experiencing unjust treatment increased steeply; those from developing countries were worst affected, suffering non-payment of already earned wages, being stranded without money in ports far from home when their companies experienced financial difficulties, and serving in sub-standard ships. The prolonged and continuing war between Iran and Iraq brought anxiety, fear and sometimes injury and death to seafarers whose ships were trading in that area.[26] And the huge increase in the numbers of Asian seafarers encouraged the Churches to try to provide more specifically Asian ministry.

Every organisation ministering to seafarers experienced these problems at first hand, and action was taken to assist seafarers. In 1981 the Seamen's Church Institute of New York and New Jersey established the Center for Seafarers' Rights; the Center's object was to deal with cases of unjust treatment of seafarers arising in ports in North America and beyond, and at the time of writing its influence is growing steadily. Side by side with this development, and to complement its work, The Missions to Seamen set up a department in its Central Office in London to correlate information received and offer advice and assistance to seafarers with specific problems. In 1985 the International Christian Maritime Association held its plenary conference in the Philippines; the object of this was to obtain an on-the-spot understanding of the life of a country which annually supplies more than 50,000 seafarers to man ships registered in other countries, and to make known its concern about the deplorable treatment some of those seafarers were receiving from a significant number of manning agencies and officials in their own country. The pastoral problems arising from the constant menace of unemployment and the Iran–Iraq War were handled by chaplaincy staff all over the world. The need to provide specifically Asian-orientated ministry within international and interconfessional chaplaincy teams was recognised, and while progress in getting Asian ministers or priests to undertake this ministry has been slow it is encouraging to note that in the Vancouver chaplaincy team working from the Flying Angel Club of The Missions to Seamen both a Korean and a Taiwanese Presbyterian minister are employed. In 1986 approximately one third of the 30,000 seafarers visiting the Vancouver centre were Asian.

On the purely denominational front there were a number of noteworthy happenings. The German Seamen's Mission widened its horizons. 'Where not so long ago they ministered only to German seafarers now they operate happily with other Societies ministering on an international basis, and their participation in the ecumenical chaplaincy at Antwerp is very much welcomed. They have given a clear lead with the project at Felixstowe, now happily operating very successfully, and their Diakon at Wilton (Middlesbrough, Teesside) has fitted very happily into the chaplaincy team based at Flying Angel House. In addition to these places . . . they have also taken the lead in working for the establishment of an international seafarers' centre in Jakarta. The Apostleship of the Sea and The Missions to Seamen have happily accepted the role played by the German Seamen's Mission with this project, and the harmonious way in which all the negotiations have been conducted augurs well for the future.'[27]

The Danish Seamen's Church sought invitations to carry out its ministry to seafarers from the premises of The Missions to Seamen in Hong Kong and Yokohama, and these were willingly and joyfully extended. The other Nordic seamen's missions continued to minister almost exclusively to Nordic seafarers and Nordic expatriate communities, and their position was understood by the other organisations.

In 1970 Pope Paul VI set up the Pontifical Commission for the Pastoral Care of Migrant and Itinerant People, attached to the Sacred Congregation of the Bishops. Its aim was 'to provide better for the spiritual welfare of those who live away from home' by setting up a single co-ordinating body, and among the ministries it was to embrace were 'the care of emigrants, the Apostleship of the Sea, the Apostleship of the Air, the Apostolate of Nomads . . .' The Commission was to 'enjoy a certain autonomy' in carrying out its functions. Its first duty was 'to deal with the pastoral care of people who are itinerant . . .' The Holy Father hoped that 'from this

Commission . . . will arise many and important pastoral benefits, and that the maternal solicitude of the Church, perceiving
the signs and needs of the times, will so much the more be
brought into light and become a gently persuasive testimony
of the Church to men.'[28] The importance of the ministry of the
Apostleship of the Sea to the Roman Catholic Church, and its
inclusion in this new Commission with its brief to care for the
spiritual welfare of all people 'on the move', provided a great
stimulus to the work of The Missions to Seamen within the
Anglican Communion.

The Anglican Missions to Seamen committed itself
wholeheartedly to interconfessional collaboration. During
this period its ministry expanded in Australia, New Zealand,
Southern Africa, the Arabian Gulf, Asia and North America. It
tried to meet new needs as they arose, and to meet them in
partnership with others. It established mobile ministries in
Toronto and Sarnia in Canada, and the British Sailors' Society
used the same idea for its work in Aberdeen and Great
Yarmouth.

Truly this was an age of change!

Notes

1. Adrian Hastings, 'A History of English Christianity 1920–85, p. 97.
2. Ewan Corlett, 'The Revolution in Merchant Shipping' 1981, p. 6.
3. Lay Reader is the title given in the Anglican Church to a lay person
    licensed by the Bishop of the Diocese to conduct public worship and
    carry out certain pastoral duties.
4. Quoted in 'Flying Angel' by L. A. G. Strong, Methuen, 1956, p. 149.
5. Ibid. p. 115.
6. Peter Anson 'The Church and the Sailor' 1948, p. 87.
7. Ibid. p. 90.
8. Ibid. p. 90.
9. Ibid. p. 92, 93.
10. Ibid. p. 97.
11. Ibid. p. 97 and 99.
12. Ibid. p. 99, 100.
13. Ibid. p. 101.
14. Ibid. p. 101.
15. Ibid. p. 101.
16. Ibid. p. 171.
17. Adrian Hastings, 'A History of English Christianity 1920–1985,'
    p. 520.

18. J. M. Roberts, 'The Pelican History of the World', p. 921.
19. Hastings, ibid. p. 525.
20. Ronald Preston, 'The testing of the Churches,' ed. Davies, p. 83.
21. The Revd. Prebendary Tom Kerfoot, General Secretary of The Missions to Seamen and later the first General Secretary of the International Christian Maritime Association.
22. Conclusions and Resolutions as agreed in plenary session of the Inter-national Consultation on Services to Seafarers; 28.8.1969. This document is available from the International Christian Maritime Association.
23. Ibid.
24. In a survey carried out by The Missions to Seamen in 1976 among its chaplaincy staff only 3 people—one an Honorary Chaplain, one a full-time chaplain and one a full-time Lay Reader—stated that they would not be prepared to work in a multidenominational chaplaincy team using one building. More than 90% said unequivocally that they would.
25. 'Flagging out' is the term applied to the process of companies registering ships in certain foreign countries in order to benefit from favourable taxation and employment regulations and conditions. Not all countries have equally high standards in matters like safety regulations and conditions of service for foreign seafarers.
26. At 20.8.88, when the ceasefire was signed there had been 547 attacks on ships in the Gulf (predominantly merchant ships but also including peace keeping forces), and 420 seafarers had been killed (including service personnel).
27. W. J. D. Down, 'The Missions to Seamen in the future' 1977.
28. Motu Proprio 'Apostolicae Caritatis', S.S. Pauli PP. VI, 19.3.1970.

IV The Shipping Scene in the Late 1980's

'All trade depends on transport. Ninety-five per cent by weight of all trade that crosses frontiers is waterborne, including inland. Over ninety-nine and a half per cent by weight of all trans-ocean cargo is carried in ships, under half a per cent in aircraft, and there is no viable alternative mode for most of it.'

British Maritime League, 1987.[1]

In the 1960's a technological revolution affecting every aspect of the shipping scene began and is still going on. In the 1970's a severe world-wide trade recession followed the astronomical rises in the price of crude oil imposed by the Arab nations, and it too is still going on. In the 1980's the pattern of ownership, registration, management and crewing of ships has been, and still is, changing fundamentally. The purpose of this chapter is to note how these and other factors have affected the shipping scene and to portray the setting in which the Churches are currently seeking to minister to the seafaring community.

The technological revolution of the 1960's was the natural outcome of concentrated research in the field of ship design and cargo transportation in a period of comparative peace following the Second World War. Contributory factors included the unexpected and prolonged closures of the Suez Canal, the continuing uncertainty over its future (which spurred the industry to design and build very much larger oil tankers and bulk carriers), and the ever-increasing cost of port labour which, coupled with the crippling effect of outdated working practices, made the development of new methods of cargo handling a top priority for the industry.

Undoubtedly the most far-reaching development on the shipping scene in the 1960's was the advent of containerisation. Containerisation is the name given to the inter-modal system

of carrying assorted dry cargo in specially constructed standard size metal boxes which can also be swiftly and mechan-
ically lifted from shore to ship and ship to shore. Before its
introduction dry cargo was brought to a port by road or rail,
unloaded into a warehouse, and stacked ready for loading.
Dockers loaded the cargo in nets or slings which were then
lifted by shore-side cranes or ships' derricks and lowered into
the ship's hold, supervised by the stevedore and the ship's
officers. Because the work was necessarily done in the open air,
and because often the cargo was perishable, severe weather
conditions seriously hindered loading. At the other end of
the voyage the process was repeated in reverse. It was an
expensive, labour-intensive, time-consuming system, rendered
unpredictable by weather conditions, the state of labour
relations, and other factors. When containerisation was
mooted it had immediate attractions for shipowners, shippers
and traders. The length of time ships would spend in port
would be drastically curtailed and could be calculated accur-
ately. Loading and discharging containers away from the port
would reduce the almost universal port scourge of pilferage,
and the enormous cost of manhandling cargo would be sub-
stantially reduced. There were also formidable deterrents.
Specialised ships would have to be built. New facilities to
handle them would have to be set up in ports wherever such
ships would call. Inland bases for loading and unloading the
containers would have to be established. A whole new concept
of integrated cargo transportation, in which the ship was just
one vital element, would be needed. It would be expensive! To
dockers and some of the other port workers it represented the
end of long-established practices, redundancies on a massive
scale, and the introduction of a new system and new skills
which had simply no place for traditional dock work. Resist-
ance was bound to be fierce. It was! But containerisation came,
and came to stay.

Its beginnings were unremarkable. In 1950 the United
Steamship Company of Copenhagen built two small container
ships to provide door-to-door service within the region. Before
then 'cargo, such as ale from Copenhagen Breweries, was
manhandled crate by crate from trucks into the holds of
coasters. The United system permitted the loading of a container with 72 crates in less than two minutes, into single holds

. . . allowing a fairly clear drop-in.'[2] The ships were very small, however, and the potential of this imaginative concept was not immediately recognised.

The real initiator of containerisation as we know it today was an American road transport operator, Malcolm Mac-Lean. His business involved moving trailers by road from one point to another within the United States of America, and in order to reduce the heavy costs of road transport he acquired a shipping company to carry his trailers by sea whenever possible. His basic idea, which was so simple as to be revolutionary, was to use ships simply as links in a comprehensive transport chain, as opposed to using subsidiary services at each end of a ship-centred system. In implementing this he reversed the traditional pattern. In 1956 he converted two tankers to carry 35 feet long trailer vans, detachable from their chassis, to operate between New York and Houston. This led on to the development of both 'roll on/roll off' (driving vehicles or detachable trailers on to a ship at one terminal and off at the other) and 'lift on/lift off' (shoreside gantry crane loading) vessels. In 1957 he converted the cargo ship 'Gateway City' into the world's first true container ship, and soon afterwards brought nine similar ships into service. 'In one brilliant leap MacLean produced an entirely new type of ship, which has changed little in principle and not really much in detail ever since.'[3] 'Gateway City' could carry 226 35 feet long containers and could be turned round in port in one day—a striking contrast with the length of time traditional cargo handling procedures would have taken.

In 1965 standard dimensions for containers were internationally agreed,[4] and the way was open for development on a world-wide scale. In 1969 Overseas Containers Ltd. (a consortium of the independent British shipping companies P & O British and Commonwealth, Alfred Holt and Furness Withy) brought the 'Encounter Bay' into service. She was the first of a fleet of six long-range deep-sea trade cellular container ships capable of carrying 1500 standard 20 feet long containers at a speed of 21.5 knots, and operated on the United Kingdom–Europe–Australia run. In the same year Associated Container Transportation introduced the first of its fleet of similar ships, and other consortia were also being formed at that time. A second class of container ships—larger and faster—quickly followed, and others were designed to handle particular trades and routes. Within twenty years of the standardising of container sizes container terminals were established in major ports all over the world.[5]

Once containerisation was fully established analysis of its impact on the shipping scene revealed that 'the rate of cargo handling in port had been speeded up by more than ten times with a third of the labour. Furthermore, the cost of cargo damage and loss was reduced to about 10 per cent of that in the break bulk[6] system, and the entire fleet operated with 10 per cent of the number of crew of the conventional ships to carry the same ton mileage per annum.'[7] To describe the impact of containerisation as revolutionary is a well justified use of an over-worked word. Further reference will be made to its effect on the manning levels of ships.

If the advent of containerisation and the introduction of the container ship was the most far-reaching development on the shipping scene in the 1960's, it was very far from being the only major one.

The closure of the Suez Canal in 1956, a prolonged closure between 1967 and 1975, uncertainty over its future, and continuing political unrest in the region, combined to force tanker operators to examine very carefully the logistics of shipping vast quantities of oil to destinations all over the world by alternative routes. The extra distance from the oil ports of the Arabian/Persian Gulf to the terminals of Western Europe using the Cape route round Southern Africa rather than the Suez Canal is approximately 4500 nautical miles[8] each way. The ships would have to spend correspondingly more days at sea, overall costs would be much higher, and fewer round voyages could be made in a year. The obvious answer was to design and build bigger tankers, and this was what happened. In 1955 the biggest tanker built was the 'Sinclair Petrolore' of 56,089 deadweight tons.[9] In 1960 the biggest was the 'Universe Daphne' of 115,000 d.w.t. In 1970 the 'Berge King' had a capacity of 280,000 d.w.t., and in 1976 the 'Oppama' (now the 'Seawise Giant') had a capacity of 564,000 d.w.t. This rapid increase in the size of tankers was accompanied by some technical problems, and at the end of the 1960's and the beginning of the 1970's there were a number of disastrous tanker explosions. Design modifications rectified these.

These huge ships, the biggest of which are more than 1500 feet long with a beam of around 210 feet and a fully laden draught of more than 90 feet, have changed the whole tanker scene. They cannot enter conventional ports because of the depth of water they require. Loading is carried out by pipelines at some distance from the shore, and discharging is by pipelines and smaller tankers. Loading and discharging are very quick, with even the biggest tanker turned round within two days. Crew members have few opportunities for shore leave at such terminals. The number of these huge ships has remained relatively small, however, partly because of the drawbacks of their size and the fear of pollution on a vast scale in the event of an accidental spillage of oil, but also because alterations to the Suez Canal now permit fully laden tankers of around 250,000 d.w.t. to pass through. Tankers of this size have proved to be the most economically viable of the ultra large crude oil carriers.

At the present time there is a serious surplus of tanker capacity in the world. There are many more tankers than there are cargoes for them to carry, and many are laid up in estuaries, bays and fjords around the world. Competition for cargoes of oil is razor sharp. Many tanker operators have been severely affected by optimistic over-ordering of ships, and a significant number of them have been bankrupted.

The factors which led to the phenomenal increase in size of oil tankers produced a similar development in bulk carriers. These are the ships which carry large quantities of dry cargo, such as coal, metal ores and grain, in bulk form. Unlike the very large tankers, however, bulk carriers usually need to berth at shoreside jetties where their cargoes can be loaded or discharged, though some are self-discharging. Their size is therefore limited by the depth of water in the ports where they operate, and few have a capacity of much more than 250,000 deadweight tons.

Around the world a number of new ports have come into being to handle recently discovered and commercially marketable resources of coal and metal ores. On the West Coast of Canada the port of Prince Rupert established new deep water facilities in the mid 1980's for the export of coal and grain. In South Africa Richards Bay, which came into being as a port in 1976 and currently exports more than 40 million tons of coal annually, can handle ships of around 250,000 deadweight tons, as can the natural deep water port of Saldanha Bay, which exports iron ore. In Western Australia new deep water ports for the export of the vast quantities of high grade iron ore discovered in the hinterland were built at Dampier and Port Walcott in the early 1970's, and the existing harbour at Port Hedland was significantly deepened and extended for the same trade. On the Eastern seabord of Australia the port of Gladstone was developed to export bauxite and coal; it too is a deep water port. Among other countries which have built new deep water ports to handle bulk cargoes are Brazil, Chile and India, and all over the world a number of existing ports have been radically developed so as to be able to accommodate large bulk carriers.

One of the problems common to the operation of tankers and bulk carriers has been the enormous distances such vessels have had to travel unladen on their way to load cargo or after discharging it. It has always been very expensive to run an unloaded ship and in recent years the combination of high fuel prices, world trade recession, a surplus of cargo carrying ships and cut-throat competition for the cargoes that were available has led to the development of multi-purpose vessels like the Oil/Bulk/Ore (O.B.O.) carrier and the (Oil) Product/Oil/Bulk/Ore (P.R.O.B.O.) carrier. These highly sophisticated ships, which can carry either liquid or dry bulk cargo, have not been without their operational problems, however, and a question mark must hang over their future.

There were revolutionary innovations in a number of other areas of seaborne cargo transportation, too, and without doubt these will play an important part in the development of the shipping industry in the future.

For many years the world's vast resources of natural gas, of which methane forms a large part of what is available, were under-utilised, except in countries like the United States and Russia. Although methane is an excellent fuel it was considered to be unusable, except when located within piping distance of substantial markets, because of its nature. 'It is a light gas, explosive when mixed with air, cannot be liquefied under pressure alone, and when carried as a refrigerated liquid boils at minus 161°C!'[10] Discovered in oil-rich areas like the Arabian/Persian Gulf, Algeria and off the coast of Western

Australia, it was either left in the ground or burned off as waste in staggering quantities—in 1978 it was estimated that the amount being burned off around the world was equivalent to approximately 75% of the gas consumption of Western Europe.[11] Clearly there were lessons to be learned from the United States and the Soviet Union, where local natural gas had for many years provided a considerable proportion of the energy supply, and a challenge existed to find a safe way of transporting this rich resource with a view to harnessing it for commercial purposes. Shipping it in liquid form had great attractions, since methane reduced in volume 630 times when liquefied, but the technical problems were immense.

In 1959 intensive research and brilliant naval architecture resulted in a cargo ship being specially converted to carry liquid natural gas. She was re-named 'Methane Pioneer'. She sailed from Louisiana to a specially built terminal at Canvey Island on the Thames. Over the next year seven further voyages were made without mishap, and the way was open for commercial expansion. In 1964 the 'Methane Princess' and a sister ship went into service between Britain and Algeria; they carried 12,000 tons of liquid natural gas at a speed of more than 17 knots. Soon the ships got bigger and more numerous. By 1980 72 Liquid Natural Gas carriers were in service and a further 26 were on order. Their future seemed assured.

The ships themselves are highly distinctive in appearance, and they represent a triumph of applied research and bold imaginative design. 'Perhaps more than any other, the Liquid Natural Gas carrier represents the sheer daring and technical expertise of shipowners and naval architects in the last quarter of a century.'[12]

A second highly distinctive type of ship was the specialised car carrier. Because motor cars are relatively light, require considerable stowage space, and were being exported in increasingly large numbers, the task of shipping them from one country or continent to another became a problem to both manufacturer and shipping company alike. The provision of sufficient satisfactory regular and reliable facilities for transporting cars on conventional ships at a mutually acceptable price was found to be impossible, and motor manufacturers moved into the business of chartering ships themselves. Soon European and Japanese manufacturers became interested in building specially designed car carriers capable of carrying large numbers of vehicles and being loaded and discharged very rapidly. The first ocean-going car carrier, which was built in Japan in 1965 and carried 1200 cars, was the 'Opama Maru'. Such ships are now a familiar sight on the oceans of the world.

A third distinctive type of ship was the Lighter Aboard Ship vessel, a commercial development of the Landing Dock Ship designed in the Second World War. The basic idea was to float barges or lighters into and out of a ballasted-down parent ship, or lift them on and off by heavy-lift shipboard cranes. The great attraction of this mode of transport was that barges or lighters, pre-loaded with cargo in one port or country, could be delivered by the ocean-going parent ship to a shallow water port in another country, and collected later (discharged and re-loaded with fresh cargo) for delivery to another port. In practice there have been real problems with the operation of this type of ship: universal standardisation of the sizes of barges and lighters was never accepted, the ships themselves were very expensive to build, and there was too much waste of space and weight. They are not as widely employed as was originally hoped.

A fourth distinctive type of ship was the much smaller offshore supply vessel. With improved technology making possible the commercial exploitation of huge reserves of oil and natural gas located under the sea in many parts of the world, a large number of rigs and drilling platforms were built for exploration and development purposes. The transportation to and from the rigs of specialised equipment, machinery and personnel required fast, flexible and reliable supply vessels, and in the 1960's highly sophisticated small vessels were brought into service to meet these needs.

The rapid development of the passenger aircraft, culminating in the introduction of the wide-bodied jet airliner, brought a virtual end to regular inter-continental passenger liner services by sea in the 1960's—to the regret and sadness of many.

The great passenger ships were switched to pleasure cruising, and this has proved to be a lucrative market. Some fine new ships have been brought into service: they include Cunard's 'Queen Elizabeth 2' in 1968 and 'Cunard Countess' and 'Cunard Princess' in 1976, P & O's 'Royal Princess' in 1984, Royal Caribbean Cruise Line's 'Song of America' in 1982 and 'Sovereign of the Seas' in 1988, and others. Competition for customers has been very keen, and the cost-cutting activities of some of the companies operating under flags of convenience have caused concern to many who have the welfare of seafarers at heart.

The passenger ferries which operate in many parts of the world have been up-graded in recent years. There was a realisation that in order to provide an attractive alternative to air travel for passengers undertaking relatively short journeys from one place to another the standard of sea travel had to be significantly improved. By and large this has happened. Passenger facilities have improved greatly and traditional methods of loading and carrying cargo and motor vehicles have been replaced by the rapid roll on/roll off facility. The speed at which the ferries travel has been increased, the comfort of the passenger has a higher priority, and the keen competition for trade has ensured that standards have improved constantly.

This brief account of the revolution which has taken place in the design of ships and the concept of seaborne cargo has to be viewed in the light of current world trading patterns if an accurate and comprehensive picture of the situation facing the Churches as they minister to today's seafaring community is to be presented.

In 1973 the oil producing countries of the Middle East were instrumental in creating a crisis in commercial circles throughout the world by imposing a series of rapid and steep increases in the price of crude oil. It rose fourfold in one year. The reverberations of their action were felt everywhere, since most countries used vast quantities of oil for domestic, industrial and transportation purposes and had become heavily dependent on it. Transport, manufacturing, food and energy supply costs rocketed up everywhere, and there was scarcely a household that was not affected in some way. The world's financial systems came under heavy strain, and it was a long time before stability was restored.

Since the end of the 1970's, and possibly as a result of the oil price crisis, a deep and prolonged trade recession has affected the world's markets, and the impact on the shipping scene has been enormous. World trade currently totals 3300 million tonnes a year[13]—an eightfold increase since 1946—and all trade depends on transport. 95% by weight of all trade that crosses frontiers is waterborne (including inland waterways), and over 99.5% by weight of all trans-ocean cargo is carried in ships. Less than 0.5% is carried in aircraft, and there is no viable alternative to seaborne transportation for most of it.[14] A world trade recession inevitably affects shipping as well as the economies and interdependence of most countries.

The effects of the oil price rise, the rush to build large tankers to profit from the demand for oil, the continuing world trade recession, and the revolution in ship design and construction, have all combined in the 1980's to change the long-established patterns of ship ownership, registration and operation.

Traditionally, the largest shipowning nations have been the industrialised countries of Western Europe, Scandinavia, the United States of America, Japan (since the Second World War) and the Soviet Union and its satellites. Now there is a steep decline in the numbers of ships owned and registered in Western Europe, Scandinavia and the United States of America, and a phenomenal and continuing increase of ships registered under flags of convenience.* In 1987 'at least 40% of the current world fleet is registered under flags of convenience',[15] and while it is true that the actual control of many ships so registered lies in Western Europe, Scandinavia and the United Sates, it is also true that the owners find it highly beneficial to operate under these flags. The major flag of convenience registries are Liberia, Panama, the Bahamas, Singapore, Cyprus and Bermuda, though increasing numbers of ships are being registered in off-shore dependencies like the Isle of Man (for the United Kingdom) and Kerguelen (for France). In 1986 the ten principal merchant fleets of the world, in terms of gross registered tonnage,[16] were:

---

* 'By the term "flag of convenience" is understood the practice of registering a ship in a country other than the one in which it is owned. This is often done to obtain more favourable tax concessions, or to avoid the stringent safety standards of the country of ownership, or to escape the attentions of trade unions over conditions of employment.' See Chapter One, Note 3.

Liberia	with	1658 ships totalling 52,649,000 g.r.t.
Panama	with	5252 ships totalling 41,305,000 g.r.t.
Japan	with	10,011 ships totalling 38,488,000 g.r.t.
Greece	with	2255 ships totalling 28,390,000 g.r.t.
U.S.S.R.	with	6276 ships totalling 24,960,000 g.r.t.
U.S.A.	with	6496 ships totalling 19,901,000 g.r.t.
United Kingdom (including the Isle of Man)	with	2256 ships totalling 11,567,000 g.r.t.
China (People's Republic)	with	1562 ships totalling 11,567,000 g.r.t.
Cyprus	with	940 ships totalling 10,617,000 g.r.t.
Norway	with	2107 ships totalling 9,295,000 g.r.t.

Ships of less than 500 gross registered tons account for approximately half the world fleet numbers, and these figures are taken from Lloyds Register of Shipping Statistical Tables.

Lloyds Register divides the major merchant fleets of the world for purposes of comparison into four groupings. These are Western Europe (the countries of the European Economic Community, together with Norway, Sweden and Finland), Flags of Convenience (Liberia, Panama, the Bahamas, Cyprus and Bermuda, but not the Isle of Man), the Pacific Basin (all countries bordering on the Pacific, except the Soviet Union and the Americas), and Comecon (Albania, Bulgaria, the German Democratic Republic, Hungary, Poland, Romania, the Soviet Union, Czechoslovakia and Yugoslavia). In 1985 the Flag of Convenience fleet overtook that of Western Europe and became the biggest grouping in terms of gross registered tonnage. In 1986 the Pacific Basin fleet also overtook Western Europe and was climbing towards the Flag of Convenience level. The Comecon group remained the smallest. Japan currently has the largest national flag (as opposed to flag of convenience) fleet, and the fleet of the People's Republic of China is growing steadily.

Alongside the decline in ownership and registration of ships in Western Europe, Scandinavia and the United States of America, and the increase of registrations under flags of convenience, there has been a far-reaching change in the pattern of ship owning itself. In the past many shipowning companies in industrialised countries concentrated almost exclusively on shipping and shipping-related commercial interests, and famous companies bore family names or had long family associations. The revolution which has affected every aspect of shipping in the last quarter of a century, necessitating the investment of huge capital sums on the one hand and cut-throat competition with a sizable number of unscrupulous ship operators on the other, led many to reduce drastically the size of their fleets, transfer their ships from national registries to flags of convenience, merge their shipping interests into consortia, and diversify their business activities into other fields. Many newly-established ship operators required huge loans to launch their companies, and many banks in the industrialised world were prepared to advance large sums. A significant number of these companies have gone out of business owing substantial sums to the banks; and the banks have also acquired substantial stakes in the ownership of new ships.

Another factor giving rise to widespread concern is the massive surplus of ships in the world. There are far too many ships competing for the cargoes that are available. It is recognised that the freight rates in most trades on every route are depressed below the point at which most ships are able to operate profitably. It is reported that U.S. $6 billion of ultra large crude (oil) carriers are currently laid up,[17] and it is estimated that before profitable trading can be restored there is a need for a reduction by one third of the total gross registered tonnage of the world's fleet.[18] Scrapping of unrequired vessels is essential. Progress is being made in this direction. But the problems are immense and the progress is slow.

This changed and changing pattern of the ownership, registration and operation of ships has resulted in fundamental changes in the manning of ships both in terms of the number of seafarers employed and also of the countries in which they are recruited. With streamlining of costs a prime consideration for all ship operators in an age of intense competition for trade, one immediate area for potential savings was the crew's wages bill. It is indisputable that it is much less expensive to employ a crew from one of the developing countries than one from any of the industrialised countries, when the latter's conditions of service are related to the cost of living in their home country and protected by strong and active trade unions. A policy document[19] published by the General Council of British Shipping in December 1987 set out the position very clearly: it stated that the average crew cost per United Kingdom-registered ship in mid 1987 was U.S. $1 million (£625,000 at the then exchange rate of $1.60—£1) per annum; crew cost saving per ship with Far East/Polish crews was $550,000 (£344,000), and crew cost saving per ship operating under Isle of Man terms was $248,000 (£155,000) per annum. Such figures speak for themselves. The decision to transfer ships from the registries of industrialised countries, where wages are high and employment is strongly protected, to flags of convenience, where crews from developing countries can be employed at greatly reduced cost and under less demanding conditions of service, was inevitable. The process had been going on since the mid 1970's, and the rate of the annual reduction in the number of seafarers from industrialised countries was alarmingly high; in the United Kingdom the reduction has been in the region of 5000 annually since 1974, and the number of seafarers undergoing training has also dropped sharply. The increase in the number of seafarers from developing countries has been correspondingly high, and in 1987 it was estimated—though no accurate comprehensive data could be discovered—that two thirds of the world's seafarers come from developing countries, mostly Asian. In 1987 the manning agencies of the Philippines, the world's largest supplier of crews for foreign-registered ships, provided more than 60,000 seafarers for mainly flag of convenience vessels—and still had some 120,000 trained seafarers anxiously awaiting jobs. For purposes of comparison it is illuminating to note that in 1987 the number of United Kingdom seafarers serving on British flag vessels was in the region of 25,000.

A feature of the current world shipping scene which is causing concern and is a direct product of world-wide trade recession, over-supply of ships and cut-throat competition for the cargoes which are available, is the sub-standard ship. By this is meant a ship which may be structurally in a dangerous state of neglect, insufficiently provided with safety equipment like life-rafts, life-jackets and life-belts, poorly maintained as regards its basic machinery, equipment and life boats, or manned by inadequately qualified or even unqualified officers. Such ships exist in relatively small but significant numbers, and examples of them will be cited later. They trade in parts of the world where they are unlikely to encounter strong official or trade union action. They are often registered under a flag of convenience. They are often manned by multi-national crews whose members come from developing countries and are desperate for any paid employment; sometimes they do not have proper contracts of service. The companies operating them sometimes change the ship's name and place of registration with bewildering frequency, and are slow to pay the crew's wages. Eventually many such ships are arrested while in port for non-payment of bills, and the owners become difficult to locate. The crew may be stranded on the ship in a port far from home, without food, fuel, money or tickets to travel home, and with large arrears of wages owed to them. It needs to be re-emphasised that such ships are not the norm; on the contrary, they form a small minority of the world's ships. But they exist in sufficient numbers to pose a real and significant problem, and seafarers' chaplains and trade union officials in many parts of the world are dealing regularly and frequently with the appalling human anguish and distress they cause. They represent a threat to the safety of the seafarers who man them and to those who encounter them. They undermine the properly conducted business of the majority of shipowners. Their operators flagrantly flout established practices of ship-owning and trading. In many ports great efforts are being made, at many levels, to track down the owners of these ships and compel them either to raise their standards to an acceptable level or discover that ports will not accept them. Port State Control, which involves inspections of foreign vessels visiting a nation's ports by government surveyors, is a very effective deterrent if applied universally, but universal application is still a long way from realisation at present.

A study of the data relating to total losses (including constructive total losses) in recent years of ships of 500 tons gross or more makes revealing reading, especially when concentrated on the flag of convenience registries. The figures which follow are extracted from tables published by the Institute of London Underwriters, with assistance from the Casualty Branch of the Intelligence Department of Lloyd's of London Press. It is emphasised that these figures are selected to illustrate points being made, but it can also be stated categorically that thorough scrutiny of comprehensive statistics, copies of which may be found as Appendix A, in no way contradicts the conclusions. Facts to bear in mind are that the three largest flag of convenience registries are Liberia, Panama and Cyprus; Japan has the largest national flag fleet; Greece, the Soviet Union, the United Kingdom and the People's Republic of China have, respectively, the fourth, fifth, seventh and eighth largest fleets; and South Korea is included because of the high number of ships of its registry which are lost. The total losses of ships of 500 g.r.t. or more for the years 1983–87 were as shown in the table (see page 78).

The figures in the column marked 1986 Total Fleet refer to the number of ships in the country's registry and their total gross registered tonnage. Approximately half of the world's registered ships are below 500 g.r.t. Certain conclusions may be drawn. Liberia has done much in recent years to improve its safety record, and its decision not to accept ships more than ten years old on its register obviously proved beneficial, though this policy has been relaxed recently. Panama has three times more ships on its register than Liberia, and the continuing high level of losses is very disquieting. Greece and Cyprus cause concern over their losses. Japan, the United Kingdom, the Soviet Union and the People's Republic of China have good records. The South Korean figures are worrying in view of the size of its fleet. And it should be said again and again that every country registering ships should do everything in its power to prevent the loss of any ship.

Another feature of the seafaring scene today is the continuing incidence of piracy. Piracy, by which is meant armed robbery at sea, has been a problem for the shipping community from time immemorial. It might have been thought, however, that with the increasing sophistication of surveillance equipment on ships, greater security of cargo with the introduction of containerisation and heavy mechanically-operated hatch covers, the constant use of radar which can detect the presence of even tiny craft (though wooden boats are not easy to spot), the increase of both the size and speed of merchant ships, and the possibility of immediate requests for assistance being transmitted and acted upon, it might now be a declining phenomenon. Such is not the case. Piracy has continued to flourish and even increase. In recent years problem areas

Ship Losses

Nationality	1983		1984		1985		1986		1987		Total Fleet 1986	
	No. Lost	G.R.T.	No. Lost	G.R.T.	No. Lost	G.R.T.	No. Lost	G.R.T.	No. Lost	G.R.T.	No. of ships	G.R.T.
Liberia	7	182,573	9	186,791	8	155,064	1	11,045	6	68,972	1,658	52 million
Panama	56	312,026	48	284,750	42	333,710	34	222,139	19	169,399	5,252	41 million
Cyprus	5	21,864	10	43,171	11	42,285	15	104,929	17	75,359	940	10 million
Japan	8	7,270	3	1,915	5	6,568	1	1,535	3	5,438	10,011	38 million
Greece	37	329,370	30	349,623	11	177,342	15	197,953	6	126,361	2,255	28 million
Soviet Union	4	13,026	4	24,229	2	11,688	2	37,405	2	13,192	6,726	25 million
United Kingdom	—	—	—	—	3	2,403	—	—	1	726	2,256	11 million
China	2	22,578	2	15,288	—	—	1	3,995	0	0	1,562	11 million
South Korea	13	45,770	9	22,423	15	86,636	11	134,382	12	150,815	1,837	7 million

have been West Africa, the narrow shipping channels of the Malacca Strait off the coasts of Singapore, Malaysia and Indonesia, the Gulf of Siam, the Sulu Sea off the Philippines, and Brazil. There have also been attacks in other areas, notably in the Caribbean and off Central America. In the years 1980 to 1984 four hundred well authenticated armed attacks on ships were recorded as having taken place,[20] and it is thought that this figure does not represent anything like the full total since often ships' masters, crews and shipping companies have sound reasons for not reporting them. In those four hundred attacks the pirates actually murdered some seafarers, and they invariably threatened or employed physical violence. Their intention was to steal money and cargo: sometimes they seemed to know exactly which containers held valuable cargo, and it was clear that they had accomplices in shipping offices and docks. They were all aware that the ship's safe is usually located in the captain's cabin. Many attacks took place on ships which were under way from powerful small craft approaching from astern in crowded waterways and under cover of darkness, thus making detection of imminent danger virtually impossible.

There are certain factors common to almost all the areas where piracy occurs. They include endemic poverty, lax security and corruption.[21] International authorities like the International Maritime Organisation (a specialist agency of the United Nations Organisation), the International Shipping Federation, and the United Nations Conference on Trade and Development, have all taken such action as they can to deal with the problem, but individual governments need to take firm action with all cases which occur in their territorial waters if significant progress is to be made.

The revolutionary changes in the design and construction of merchant ships, the introduction of new methods of cargo handling, the altered pattern of world trade, the continuing rapid growth of flag of convenience registries, and the rise in the number of seafarers from developing countries accompanied by the decrease in the numbers from industrialised countries, have all been noted. How these changes have affected the lives and conditions of service of seafarers is assessed in the remainder of this chapter.

In 1987 the International Christian Maritime Association, the organisation with which all the major Christian denominations ministering to seafarers are voluntarily associated, carried out a survey among seafarers through its member bodies in ports throughout the world. 4525 seafarers from 98 countries assisted by answering thirty questions. 52% of those interviewed were Asian, a reasonable figure in view of their current share of seafaring employment. They were advised that their answers would be treated in confidence, and they were not asked to give either their own names or the names of their ships and employers. Members of the chaplaincy staff at seafarers' centres in every continent conducted the survey and made every effort to ensure that all the questions were fully understood. The answers to the questions were enlightening —the more so since no other organisation has ever been in a position to carry out such a survey among the seafarers of the world—and will be considered together with other evidence as the effects of change are assessed. It should be borne in mind that the picture such surveys portray is necessarily limited since it can convey the views only of the small cross-section of the community contacted, but it should also be stated that few seafarers' chaplains were surprised by the conclusions; they bear out what many were thinking.

It is beyond dispute that conditions on board most ships have improved steadily in recent years. The accommodation provided for all crew members on modern ships of most types is basically very good, and many owners have included excellent leisure and recreational facilities in their planning. The quality and quantity of food provided is good, and many modern ships have a well equipped small hospital. Modern ships are fitted with an impressive range of up-to-date navigation and safety aids—the advent of radar, satellite navigation, sophisticated radio communications and echo-sounding depth gauges added a new dimension to safe navigation—and many of the heavy routine jobs which crew members performed manually are now automated. Over the last thirty years progress has been such that automation of the engine room allows the engineer on watch at night to be on stand-by in his cabin rather than on watch in the engine room for the whole time. Sophisticated methods of cargo handling, particularly on container ships, tankers, bulk carriers, car carriers and roll on/roll off vessels, have fundamentally changed the roles of crew members during their stay in port.

The effect of this comprehensive progressive modernisation has been to reduce greatly both the time specialised ships spend in port and also the number of seafarers required to man them. Modern ships spend far more time at sea and far less time in port than their predecessors. With containerisation came the concept of the 'general purpose' seafarer as opposed to the specifically deck or engine room crew member. With the reduction of the number of crew employed came a change in the pattern of the social life of a ship; fewer people are off-duty at any one time, the seafarer has more time to himself, and the perennial problems of loneliness, boredom and frustration rear their ugly heads. With the world trade recession and fierce competition for cargoes came strong pressure on the ship's personnel to get the ship to its destination at the required time regardless of any problems involved. With the introduction of specialised ships came an opportunity for many seafarers, particularly those from industrialised countries, to be accompanied by their wives on a regular basis; the lengths of voyages were reduced, and leave periods between voyages were extended. These last changes were warmly welcomed when they were introduced, but their effect has been offset in recent years by the 'flagging out'* which economic pressure has precipitated, the employment of cheaper crews from developing countries, and the consequent sharp decrease in the number of seafarers from industrialised countries being employed.

These general observations are apparent to any student of the maritime scene, and it is illuminating to see how these developments and their implications affect today's seafarers. Some of the questions put to seafarers by those carrying out the International Christian Maritime Association's survey were very penetrating and the answers given particularly revealing. On the question of the 'Flag of the ship' in which they were serving, 39% were on ships registered under the 'Flag of convenience' countries of Liberia, Panama, Cyprus, the Bahamas and Bermuda. To the question, 'Why did you go to sea?',

* 'Flagging out' is the term applied to the process of companies registering ships in certain foreign countries in order to benefit from favourable taxation and employment regulations and conditions. Not all countries have equally high standards in matters like safety regulations and conditions of service for foreign seafarers.

47% replied that it was either their chosen career or because of a love of the sea, while 43% said that it was because they either needed a job or that it paid good money. The tendency to go to sea purely to have a job and earn some money was strongest, not surprisingly, among seafarers from developing countries, and the concept of professionalism was strongest among the Burmese, Germans, Indians, Japanese, Singaporeans, British, North Americans and Yugoslavs. To the question, 'Have you been fairly treated during your time at sea?' 75% replied in the affirmative and 21% in the negative. It was deliberate policy not to suggest to seafarers ways in which they might have been unjustly treated. Of those who replied in the negative, 65% did not specify in what ways they had been unfairly treated, and of those who were specific, 10% had had problems over wages, overtime pay and family allotments; only a tiny number complained of racial discrimination. To the question, 'For how long on this trip have you signed on?', 40% indicated that it was for a period of up to 6 months, 18% for between 6 months and 1 year, 25% for between 1 and 2 years, and 1.5% for between 2 and 3 years. To the question 'Did you have to pay or are you paying someone for your present job?', more than 75% of the seafarers questioned replied in the negative. Of the 16% who said that they had paid a fee to a manning agency or some other 'middle man', it is known that many paid a sum of around U.S. $1000, which on some ships could represent more than three months wages.

One of the most significant facts to emerge from the replies was that 75% of those questioned were satisfied that they had been fairly treated during their time at sea. This reflects reasonably well on the overall balance which has been achieved in good labour relations, and it confirms the view already propounded that it is a small but significant number of ship operators who treat seafarers unjustly and take advantage of the desperate need of some of them for employment. In making the serious charge that some ship operators have treated or are treating seafarers unjustly it is right and proper to back up the charge with specific examples. Those that follow are selected from a thick file of thoroughly checked and well authenticated reports received over a considerable period of time.

From Mombasa, in March 1984, the chaplain of The Missions to Seamen wrote:

'The German captain and Chief Engineer of the m.v.
"Kisima" asked the Mission for help, as they had not been
paid for three months. The "Kisima" is a Somalia flag vessel,
owned by a Somalia/German concern. On investigation it
was discovered that she had been re-named. She was previously called the "Goverport" (same owners, Panama flag),
and as such had been the cause of a similar problem last
year. After contacting the International Transport Workers
Federation I took the Captain to the Marine Lawyer, and the
ship is now under arrest.'[24]

From Port of Spain, Trinidad, in September 1984, the
Warden of The Missions to Seamen wrote:

'We first heard of the m.v. "Free Star", an Anguillan flag 200
ton coaster, from a Swedish crew member. The full details
are long and involved, but boil down to no food, no water,
no pay and the ship is falling apart. Captain and crew were
having the same problems. She had a cargo for Barbados
and after an inspection of the vessel with the Shipping
Master, it was decided that the best thing was to allow her to
sail, after ensuring she had food and water, etc. The problem
was that if she had been arrested here the crew would have
received nothing, and cargo and ship would have rotted.
The cargo was boxes marked "Barbados Products", so it
was unlikely to sell here. The decision was one that neither
the Shipping Master nor I enjoyed, as the ship was appalling.
I put my foot through the wooden deck in one place, and the
rain came in everywhere. But the response we have had from
the Honorary Chaplain in Barbados and the authorities
there has been marvellous. The ship will be inspected and
arrested there on arrival. The owner and most of the crew
live in Barbados, and the Guyanese crew members are more
confident of repatriation with pay from there.'[25]

And, under the headline 'Mission aids crew of rotting ship',
the Editor of Flying Angel News, (the official publication of
The Missions to Seamen, wrote in March/April 1988:

'Holes in the rusty hull, faulty lifeboats, rotting deck venti-
lators, pumps not working, contaminated drinking water

and fuel tank leaking into crew accommodation. This was the list of faults found by U.K. government inspectors when they went on board the Cyprus-registered vessel 'Sarjo' in Seaham on the U.K.'s north-east coast. The crew had been so afraid for their safety after a terrifying voyage from Greece that when they got to Seaham they asked for help from The Missions to Seamen student assistant Richard Howard as soon as he visited the vessel. Richard invited the bosun to Seaham's small ecumenical centre to telephone the International Transport Workers Federation. This resulted in a representative coming to inspect the vessel. What he found prompted him to call in Government inspectors who immediately impounded the ship on the grounds that it was unseaworthy. According to the 'Sarjo's' crew they had to try to plug the holes in the ship with cement because water had poured into the ship when it sailed through the Bay of Biscay. Fears for their safety were heightened by the fact that a ship owned by the same company had sunk in the Bay of Biscay with the loss of nine lives only twelve months previously. The state of the vessel, which had been inspected and approved by Lloyd's Register only days before it sailed for Seaham, raised immediate anxiety and questions about the way ships are classified for insurance, and Lloyd's Register promised that the incident would be investigated.'[26]

No sketch of the current world shipping scene, however brief, would be complete without reference to the traumas caused by the Iran/Iraq War, which ended after eight years in August 1988. Hundreds of attacks employing the latest weaponry were made on neutral merchant ships by both sides. The attacks came suddenly and unexpectedly. Damage to ships was extensive and severe. More than 400 seafarers from many parts of the world were killed, and many more were injured.[27] The effect of the attacks on the morale of seafarers whose ships passed through the Straits of Hormuz and entered the waters of the Arabian/Persian Gulf was absolutely devastating. Seafarers' chaplains had a vital pastoral role to fulfil. At the time of writing there is real hope that this dreadful conflict has at last ended, and the seafarers of the world will be profoundly relieved and grateful if this is the case.

Notes

1. Memorandum submitted by the British Maritime League to the Transport Committee of the House of Commons on March 11 1987. It is recorded in the Minutes of Evidence of the House of Commons Transport Committee published by Her Majesty's Stationery Office on p. 185 and dated 11.3.87.
2. Ewan Corlett, 'The Revolution in Merchant Shipping, 1950–1980', p. 10, Her Majesty's Stationery Office, 1981.
3. Ibid. p. 11.
4. The International Standards Organisation sizes are based on an 8 feet by 8 feet cross section and a 20 feet length module. The standard container dimensions are 20' × 8' × 8' but they can be 10', 20' or 40' in length. See Ewan Corlett 'The Revolution in Merchant Shipping 1950–1980' p. 12.
5. In visiting the work of The Missions to Seamen in ports all over the world the writer has noted in the 1980's the introduction of container facilities in many developing countries, like Tanzania, Sri Lanka, Mozambique and others. In a visit to Shanghai in 1986 he noted the recent introduction of containerisation there.
6. Non containerised dry cargo.
7. Ewan Corlett, Ibid. p. 13.
8. 'A nautical mile is traditionally defined as the length of a minute of the arc of a great circle of the earth, but as this length varies at different latitudes, owing to the fact that the earth is not a perfect sphere, it has been rounded off at 6080 feet (1.15 land miles or 1.85 kilometres)' Information provided by the Guinness Book of Ships and Shipping, published by Guinness Superlatives Limited, 1983, p. 248.
9. Dead weight tonnage—'The actual lifting capability of a ship' (Ewan Corlett, 'The Revolution in Merchant Shipping 1950–1980).
10. Corlett, Ibid. p. 39.
11. Ibid. p. 39.
12. Ibid. p. 43.
13. British Maritime League Memorandum (see Note 1) of 11.3.1987, p. 185.
14. Ibid. p. 185.
15. Ibid. p. 187.
16. Gross registered tonnage—a measure of the internal volume of a ship.
17. British Maritime League Memorandum Ibid. p. 201.
18. Ibid. p. 199.
19. The Future of the British Merchant Fleet: An Analysis of Policy Options, published by the General Council of British Shipping, December 1987.
20. R. Villar, 'Piracy Today', published by Conway Maritime Press 1985, p. 7.
21. Ibid. p. 22.
22. See note 20.

23. 'Seafarers' Survey', The International Christian Maritime Association, 1988.'
24. Opening address, Conference on the Legal Rights of Seafarers: Nautical Institute of London—W. J. D. Down 1985, p. 1.
25. Ibid. pp. 1, 2.
26. Flying Angel News, March/April 1988.
27. At 10.8.88 when the ceasefire was signed the total number of attacks on ships, predominantly merchant ships, was 547. 420 seafarers, including service personnel, had lost their lives.

V The Church's Ministry to Seafarers
Today (A)

Practical and Pastoral, Evangelistic, Inter-confessional

'For us mission is what God is doing in the shipping world'
A seafarer's chaplain, 1976[1]

In 1976—when the effects of the revolution in ship design and
cargo handling were becoming established facts, the world
was still reeling from the astronomical oil price rises imposed
by the producer countries of the Middle East, and the
ecumenical movement was beginning to blossom in the maritime ministry of the Churches—The Missions to Seamen (the
Anglican Church's outreach to the seafaring world) sent out a
searching questionnaire to the members of its chaplaincy staff
throughout the world. The aim was to draw out their individual and collective knowledge, experience, insight, wisdom
and vision about current and future developments in the
ministry to seafarers, and incorporate these in a comprehensive
policy for the future. In reply to a question about the future
shape of his work one chaplain said that 'it is the industry
which writes the agenda for our work, and so long as we
remain adaptable to change and new opportunities as they
occur . . . our ministry will remain valid in the context of
seafaring life.'[2]

A willingness to grapple with the implications of fundamental changes in the shipping world and the ability to
come to terms with many of them has been the hallmark of the
maritime ministry of the Churches in recent years. Successive
conferences and consultations of individual denominational
and non-denominational organisations, and regional and
plenary conferences of the International Christian Maritime
Association, have all seen the provision of relevant and
appropriate ministry to seafarers as a top priority. Opportunities to establish new work have been discussed, agreed and

undertaken jointly. There is a sense of common purpose among the personnel of the individual organisations: they minister in the name of Jesus Christ to all seafarers regardless of race, rank, religion, ideology or any other consideration. There is a basic underlying goodwill towards each other among them: they pray together, they plan together and they work together. A strong bond of unity exists between them. Naturally there are some areas where progress has been slower than others, but in general the picture is exciting and encouraging.

The nature of the Church's ministry to seafarers today is complex and diverse. Those involved in it must take account of the different cultures, living standards, life styles, languages and religious affiliations of the seafarers with whom they come into contact. They must take account of the layout of the port at which a ship has arrived, the proximity and amenities of the nearest town, the length of time the ship will stay in port, the presence or otherwise of a seafarers' centre, and the availability of transport for the members of the crew. They must be sensitive to the individual needs of seafarers and know to whom to turn for particular services. They must be conversant with the workings of the shipping world. In order to present a comprehensive and comprehensible picture of it the nature of this multi-faceted ministry will be discussed under seven major headings.

Practical and Pastoral

'This is practical Christianity at work.'
H.R.H. The Duke of Edinburgh, at the opening of the new
seafarers' centre, The Missions to Seamen at Tilbury in 1956

In the course of his work the seafarer is away from home for long periods of time. He or she experiences the problems of loneliness, boredom, frustration and danger which have affected seafarers in varying degrees ever since ships first sailed across the seas. In a foreign country, and in some ports in his own country, he is a stranger. He may not speak the language.

Nevertheless he may want to go ashore to stretch his legs, get away from shipboard routine for a while, see something of the town or city he has come to, have a meal or a drink in congenial surroundings, or telephone home. Achieving all he wants to do may not be easy. His ship may be berthed a long way from the dock gate, and even further from the town. The weather may be unpleasant. He may not have much time available. He may not have enough money to pay for a taxi and the other things he wants to do. He may not have any local currency at all. It is at his point of need that the Church meets him.

When the Churches accepted that they had a responsibility to minister to seafarers they soon realised that it was right and proper for them to provide what seafarers legitimately wanted as well as what they themselves felt they should offer. They saw that they must minister to the whole person and not just to his spiritual needs. A seafarer looking forward to relaxing after a long, stressful, tedious or unpleasant voyage ought to be able to do so in comfortable surroundings, safe from the attentions of the scroungers, hangers-on and prostitutes who frequent dockside bars, eating places and clubs. A seafarer wanting good reading material to take on board ought to be able to know where to obtain it. A seafarer keen to meet fellow seafarers from other ships or ordinary decent local people ought to have a suitable meeting place available to him other than a bar or restaurant. And a Christian seafarer eager for the company and fellowship of other Christians ought to be able to know where to meet them. The Churches set out to meet these and other needs.

In many ports of the world, as has already been noted, the Churches' organisations ministering to seafarers established centres, residential hostels or clubs where all seafarers were welcome. At first what they provided was very basic, but as ships and the whole shipping scene changed and developed so too did the centres and amenities offered by the Churches. Today's seafarers' centres are imaginatively laid out, attractively decorated, well equipped and furnished, and designed to be comfortable and easy to supervise.

Seafarers' centres provided by the Churches and Christian voluntary organisations are to be found in ports around the world. They vary in size and in the nature and scope of the facilities they offer according to the size and activity of the port

they serve and the climate which prevails. A significant minority provide residential accommodation. Most provide recreational amenities, such as table tennis, billiards, television
and videos. In tropical climates some have swimming pools.
They have comfortable lounge accommodation and refreshment facilities; some have full restaurants. There is usually a
shop where a seafarer can purchase souvenirs or basic goods
required on board, change foreign currency after the banks
have closed and make arrangements for a long distance or
international telephone call.

The telephone is a vital piece of equipment. The Seafarers'
Survey carried out in 1987 by the International Christian
Maritime Association revealed that 22% of the seafarers
questioned regularly keep in touch with home by telephone,
40% by a combination of telephone calls and letters, and 62%
use the telephone as an occasional link with their families.
Statistics from Seafarers' Centres endorse the validity of these
figures: it is not uncommon for a busy centre to handle up to
10,000 international calls a year for seafarers. Privacy is
important for telephoning, and the telephone booths in a
seafarers' centre are normally equipped with a chair and a
ledge on which to write. Calls are automatically timed and the
seafarer pays after his call. Where else can a man with only
foreign money telephone home late in the evening?

All seafarers' centres have a chapel or quiet room where a
seafarer can think or meditate or pray, join in an organised
service, or make his confession. Bibles and Christian publications in various languages are available, there are plentiful
supplies of paperback books and magazines for seafarers to
take on board, and posters and other notices display information. The administration is based on Christian principles, and
many of the helpers are volunteers who willingly and regularly
make time available to provide a Christian welcome and
service to seafarers. The aim of the Churches' seafarers' centres
is to provide a Christian home-away-from-home where all
seafarers will feel welcome and experience the love of Christ in
action.

Seafarers make great use of these centres. Out of the 4525
seafarers interviewed in the International Christian Maritime
Association's survey of seafarers conducted in 1987 87%
indicated that they visit them. Of the 10% who said that they

do not visit them, lack of time available and ignorance of their existence and location were the reasons most commonly advanced. But popular and well used though the centres are, the Churches have never seen the provision of them as an end in itself. Seafarers' centres exist not only to cater for the legitimate needs of seafarers but also to provide a base for a comprehensive ministry to the whole seafaring community.

Much pastoral ministry is carried out in seafarers' centres. By pastoral ministry is understood the Church's corporate and individual calling to care about people, to be sensitive to their needs and to live out everywhere and at all times its practical commonsense concern for them. The whole team of helpers at a centre may be involved in different ways at different times. The driver of the centre's minibus may find himself listening to an anxious seafarer pouring out a problem with which he needs immediate assistance; he will either advise him himself or take him to someone better able to help. The staff member serving in the canteen or bar may be a sympathetic audience for a seafarer who is lonely, depressed, upset, or feeling that the world is against him. The woman volunteer running the shop may suddenly find herself faced by a distressed seafarer who has just telephoned home and discovered problems. Women play a key role in ministry to seafarers: they bring a wholeness and an extra dimension to a predominantly male-orientated community, and in times of crisis their presence and contribution is indispensable. Underpinning all the busyness and activity is the regular worship of the chaplain and his helpers in the chapel: there everything is laid at the Lord's feet.

Vital pastoral ministry is carried out in seafarers' centres, but much of it could not happen if the daily routine of ship visiting was not faithfully undertaken. Ship visiting is fascinating and rewarding. It is good to meet the people on a ship, see old friends and make new ones, find out where the ship has been and where it is going, share the joys and sorrows, catch up on the news, arrange the vital matter of transport to and from the centre, provide a useful service of maps, information and book exchange, and struggle with language difficulties—to the amusement of all! Relationships with seafarers are established quickly and develop over the years, and word of good seafarers' centres gets around quickly. If there are problems on board—like non-payment of wages, unsafe conditions,

serious illness, or the lingering unease after a death on board
—the chaplain or lay visitor soon hears about them and is
expected to advise and help. Sometimes he is invited to have a
meal on board; if he accepts, it is often the case that somebody
will ask him why he does what he does, and he can speak about
his faith.

As he visits ships the chaplain or lay visitor establishes
contact with people in other sections of the port's life. Harbour
officials, Customs, Port Health, Immigration, Security, trade
union officials, ships' agents, ships' chandlers, dock workers,
tug crews and lightermen are all part of his concern. He
discovers people who speak various languages and who are
prepared to help—a godsend when there is a seaman in
hospital who cannot speak the local language and therefore
cannot talk about his illness. He discovers for himself the
indefinable but very real bond which links all whose lives are
bound up with ships and seafaring.

The practical and pastoral aspect of maritime ministry is
well illustrated by a report a Lay Warden of The Missions to
Seamen submitted to the Clergy Council of his diocese in the
West Indies. He wrote:

'I would like to describe here some of the problems and some
of the other events we have been involved in over the last
month. They sound practical, and often they are, but all
involved know that Christ directs all we do, and they know
that we help them to show Christ's love for all men.

1. A Chilean seaman stranded on the wharf—we found
him a job.
2. A Ghanaian seaman in trouble with Immigration
through no fault of his own was jailed. We were able to find
help through our Church and he is now free and on a ship.
3. A ship caught fire and was gutted. The owner tried to
send the crew home without payment, but we were able to
link with the people who could bring pressure on him . . .
and the crew was paid and repatriated.
4. A seaman whose wife had left him. He had no money to
phone home. We were able to put him in touch with his wife
and the problem was resolved.
5. A seaman with spiritual problems requested to speak to a
priest—we were able to arrange for him to see one.

6. Ships' crews in port who wanted Roman Catholic or Anglican services on board—we were able to arrange them.
7. Our chapel is used ecumenically, and we were able to have an Anglican Eucharist on Christmas Eve and a Roman Catholic Mass on Christmas morning.
8. A Buddhist joined us for a service and was shown God's glory in the Eucharist.
9. A vessel arrived here with no food, no water, no pay, no safety (i.e. lifeboats, life jackets, etc.) no lighting, and rats on board. We were able to link with the Harbour Master's office and give the crew some protection.
10. A vessel sank off St. Vincent—we linked with our Honorary chaplain on Bequia, and he checked the crew was alright.'[3]

And in the trauma of the Iran/Iraq War the words of a Lay Chaplain are very appropriate:

'Any ship of any size anywhere in the Gulf is a target . . . the war is the major preoccupation of the seafarers; they all want to talk about it, to express their anger at becoming targets, for every one of them sees himself as just that—a target . . . they are innocent parties going about their everyday jobs, jobs that are already fraught with danger . . . I offer a shoulder and an ear.'[4]

Evangelistic

'Go to all peoples everywhere and make them my disciples'
St. Matthew chapter 28 verse 19.

The first assessment of maritime ministry which many Christians make is that it is practical and pastoral—and little more. Such a view is shallow. Closer scrutiny reveals a very different picture. While it is perfectly true that the very nature of seafaring requires that the Church should provide a comprehensive practical and pastoral ministry—and this is what the observer sees immediately—it is equally true that the

Churches have always seen the primary object of this ministry as being the spiritual and moral, as well as the material, well-being of seafarers. This concern to minister to the whole person is based on the belief that Jesus Christ is the Way, the Truth and the Life for all people and that in Him supremely God is manifest. The Church's calling in the martime world is, and always has been, to proclaim the Good News of Jesus Christ for all people by word and action and quality of life, to make people aware of the reality and presence of God and of the significance of Jesus, and to make disciples of all people.

Proclaiming the gospel among seafarers by word of mouth has always presented practical problems. The immediacy and brevity of many contacts between chaplains and seafarers, whose ships are in and out of port very quickly, often prevents discussion of personal matters. Meeting seafarers in groups in a lounge, duty mess or cabin sometimes keeps conversation at a superficial level. Differences of language can be daunting: if two people do not understand each other's language meaningful communication in depth through the spoken word is impossible. And the quick turn round of ships in port, the different times when ships arrive and depart, the smaller number of crew members, shipboard duties, and the distance from a ship to the seafarers' centre chapel or a local church all combine to make well-attended chapel services, with a consequent opportunity to preach, unusual.

But practical difficulties of one kind or another exist in every sort of ministry. The challenge lies in facing and overcoming them. Effective communication between people occurs most naturally when a relationship of mutual trust and confidence exists, and in the maritime world the visible presence of the Church for more than 150 years through the activities of seafarers' chaplains and the work of seafarers' centres has established a strong bond of mutual respect and good will between the Church and the seafarer.

Where individuals have a common language the Gospel can be, and is, communicated by the spoken word. Words of greeting and parting can be important. A discussion with a seafarer in his cabin, where photographs and personal items reveal something of his background, can provide an opportunity for witness. A meal with a group of seafarers often leads to questions as to why the Church does what it does. Even the simple service of supplying local information and practical assistance can mean a great deal to a stranger in a strange place and provide an opportunity to say why it is being done. Every member of the team in a Christian seafarers' centre has a vital role to play in offering a ministry of welcome and witnessing to his or her faith.

However it is not by word of mouth alone that the Gospel is communicated in the seafaring community. It is communicated by actions. Practical actions, such as driving seafarers from their ships to the seafarers' centre and back again later, taking them in the centre's minibus for a sporting fixture or a tour of the local countryside or sights, taking books to a ship or to a sick seafarer in hospital or jail, and many other similar activities, often cause seafarers to ask why Christians act as they do. The Chaplain of The Missions to Seamen in Fremantle, Western Australia, reported that:

'At the Annual General Meeting of The Missions to Seamen in Bunbury this year, an Australian seafarer with a stubbie (a can of beer) in his hand interrupted the meeting by almost falling off his stool and asking Bishop Jamieson, "Why do you do this for seafarers?" The Bishop, a former chaplain of the Royal Australian Navy replied, "Because God loves you!" The seafarer was speechless!'[5]

Actions are sometimes more powerful than words.

The Gospel is communicated by quality of life. A dedicated Christian life is a most effective instrument of evangelism. Basic moral integrity, a disciplined lifestyle, a healthy outlook on life underpinned by a simple but deep faith, and a respect for others which does not seek to force personal convictions on them, all combine to make a powerful witness to the love and care of Christ and His Church. A committed Christian is soon recognised for what he or she is. In the seafaring community, and in particular on a ship, a Christian seafarer lives his faith under the daily scrutiny of people who see his every action and hear his every word, on duty and off duty. It is a real challenge to be a Christian on a ship.

The Gospel is also communicated by the written word. Most seafarers' centres have Bibles available in various languages. Usually they are placed on a table just inside or outside the chapel, and the seafarer can take one without questions being asked. In one centre a seafarer from a Communist bloc country picked up two Bibles in his own language. He told the chaplain that he intended to take them to a congregation in his country, where few Bibles were printed. There the Bibles would be carefully taken apart, and each page would be put between two sheets of stiff plastic. Then the individual pages would circulate among the members of the congregation. That seafarer knew the power of the Word of God, and he was prepared to risk a lot to take Bibles home. It is a fact that many seafarers take a Bible in their own language from seafarers' centres.

In a community where differences of race, language, creed and culture are everyday realities, it is important for the Church to proclaim the Gospel in as many, varied and imaginative ways as possible. Just as the worship of God involves every human faculty, so the Church appeals to every human faculty as it proclaims its Lord in the seafaring community. In the design of a seafarers' centre, therefore, the prime consideration is that the seafarer's whole being should be uplifted. Decor, lighting, furnishing, equipment and layout are vital ingredients in this aim. Visual symbols of God's presence are important—an illuminated cross on the outside identifies a building for what it is; a striking picture, carving or sculpture can lift a person out of his everyday concerns, the first impression of the chapel as a place set apart and yet welcoming adds an extra dimension to the whole building, and a cross or crucifix, the stations of the Cross, an ikon, pictures and a light above the reserved sacrament can all be powerful pointers to the presence of God and the Crucified and Risen Jesus. The scent and beauty of flowers can lift a person's spirits and point him to their Creator. Good music is an effective witness—a marvellous Tanzanian choir makes a great contribution to the ecumenical worship at the seafarers' centre in Dar es Salaam. And seafarers' chaplains are aware of the value of the ministry of touch or physical contact—often it is just not possible to communicate love, care, sympathy and concern by the spoken word, especially if there is a language barrier; then the arm round the shoulder, the holding of a sick person's hand, or the touch of comfort to a grieving family, can be far more effective than words.

In the seafaring world every opportunity to preach the Gospel needs to be taken, however it occurs. An Australian chaplain of The Missions to Seamen took his opportunity like this:

'A Taiwanese bulk carrier was stopped as unseaworthy by Australian government surveyors and has since been here two weeks while repairs commence. Lifeboats unusable, also fire hoses. Hatches faulty—decks flaking up in rust. Crew accommodation disgraceful. This is the fourth such case in my time here; same company each time. Captain has been fined—company should be too!'

Crew very dispirited. I took some of them with me when I visited a country parish to preach at its harvest festival. It got them away from their problems for a while![6]

Inter-Confessional

'How good and how pleasant for brothers to worship together!'

Psalm 133, verse 1.

Without doubt one of the most striking features of the maritime ministry of the late 1980's is inter-confessional collaboration. It is a reality. The happy way in which Anglicans, Roman Catholics, Lutherans and Christians of many denominations worship, consult, discuss, pray, plan and work together is a source of inspiration and encouragement as the Churches struggle towards the unity which Our Lord Jesus Christ wills for his Church.

It was the establishment of the International Christian Maritime Association in 1969 which gave real impetus to inter-confessional collaboration in maritime ministry. At the International Consultation on Seafarers' Welfare in Rotterdam which brought it into being in that year there was a spontaneous and unanimous conviction that the way forward for the Churches in the maritime world was together in partnership. Unquestionably the Holy Spirit was working among the participants in that memorable consultation, but it is illuminating also to be aware of the reasons which brought them together and led up to their momentous conclusion and decision.

The ecumenical movement in the Churches, which had received a giant thrust forward from Pope John XXIII and the Second Vatican Council, was flourishing. There was a real belief among Christians of all denominations that progress towards unity could be achieved. The revolution in ship design and cargo handling was radically changing the whole shipping and seafaring scene. Duplication of effort and facilities in maritime ministry was recognised as being a misuse of resources. The possibility of closer collaboration with secular organisations concerned with the welfare of seafarers was felt to be worth exploring. There was increasing goodwill and respect for each other among chaplains of all denominations ministering to seafarers. And common sense pointed inexorably to the need for the Churches to take positive action to cope with the financial implications of far-reaching changes in the maritime world and Church life.

With the establishment of the International Christian Maritime Association one of its main objects—the promotion of inter-confessional collaboration—was swiftly and energetically pursued. In various parts of the world chaplains of different denominations began to work out together how they could collaborate. No one denomination or Society could be said to have been the leader, and some examples of how individual partnerships were formed and developed illustrate this.

In Antwerp, in the early 1970's, a wise and experienced Roman Catholic priest brought together the chaplains of the Anglican Missions to Seamen, the Lutheran German Seamen's Mission and the undenominational British Sailors' Society. He invited them to consider disposing of their individual seafarers' centres and working from the premises of the Apostleship of the Sea, which would be re-named the Antwerp Seafarers' Centre. Together they could plan, finance, build and operate a second centre in the newly developing container terminal. It is a measure of the stature of all the chaplains involved that they were able to convince their Bishops, ecclesiastical authorities, management committees, Society leaders and trustees that the way forward in Antwerp was together, under one roof, and as partners in ministry. The second centre was planned, built and operated together. The basic agreement between the Societies was deliberately kept simple, and the principle emerged of all the organisations being guests in a building owned and managed by one of them, and equal partners in the ministry. It was a sensible solution which maintained the legal rights and obligations of ownership while allowing full partnership and collaboration in ministry.

In Brisbane, in the early 1970's, the Anglican and Roman Catholic port chaplains became good friends. After many discussions it seemed right to them to propose to their people that they should work together from the excellent premises of The Missions to Seamen, which would be re-named the Brisbane Seafarers' Club. The Anglican and Roman Catholic Archbishops gave their consent and blessing, as did the Committee of Management of The Missions to Seamen. The chaplains then arranged a series of joint retreats and quiet days for their voluntary helpers so that they could get to know and understand each other and think positively about their new partnership. The partnership proved to be a great success, and, when a new port was built on the opposite side of the river, the Brisbane Port Authority invited The Missions to Seamen and the Apostleship of the Sea to operate jointly a new seafarers' centre there which the Port Authority would design in consultation with them and finance in its entirety. The invitation was accepted, and when the new centre was completed the voluntary workers who manned it were recruited from the local Anglican and Roman Catholic parishes.

In Felixstowe in England, in the mid 1970's, the British Sailors' Society and the German Seamen's Mission took the lead in establishing a seafarers' centre in this rapidly developing and increasingly important port. They were supported financially and in other ways by the Apostleship of the Sea and The Missions to Seamen, and a Dutch organisation, the Netherlands Seamen's Welfare Society, was also involved. In this completely new venture each participating organisation contributed equal capital sums to initiate the project, and accepted equal liability in the event of there being debts outstanding on closure. The individual organisations each provided and financed their own member(s) of the chaplaincy team, and the salaries of the domestic staff and the running costs of the centre were met from the centre's revenue from trade. Initially the leadership of the chaplaincy team was the responsibility of the German Seamen's Mission, and the management of the centre was in the hands of the British Sailors' Society, but the goodwill and positive attitudes of all the partners have allowed relationships to develop and change. The principle of equal financial commitment and responsibility represents a valuable and important guideline, though in practice a degree of flexibility over finance has had to be allowed.

In Houston in Texas it was the initiative of a group of lay business people of various denominations which led to the provision of the magnificent Houston International Seamen's Center in 1972. They saw the need for a spacious well equipped centre in this busy port which would be open to seafarers of all countries and backgrounds, and together they raised the necessary finance. They then invited the Churches to run it, and stipulated that it must operate on an ecumenical basis. The Churches accepted the invitation, and individually the members of the chaplaincy team are supported financially and in other ways by their own Churches.

These four examples of inter-confessional collaboration, which are drawn from a total of something like a hundred similar operations all over the world, are cited as illustrations of the rapidity with which inter-confessional collaboration spread once it became an accepted and acceptable policy. It should be noted, however, that some time before the establishment of the International Christian Maritime Association in 1969, The Missions to Seamen and the British Sailors' Society had sold their separate centres in Fremantle in Western Australia and built a new one together. It opened in 1967, but at that time the Apostleship of the Sea did not feel able to join them.

Since the establishment of the International Christian Maritime Association inter-confessional collaboration has spread all over the world in the maritime ministry, and reference to this can be found elsewhere in this book.* It is sufficient at this

---

* Notably in Chapter Seven, 'The International Christian Maritime Association', Chapter Eight, 'The Extent and Variety of Maritime Ministry Today' and Chapter Nine, 'On Course together'.

point to say that inter-confessional collaboration is a reality in many ports now and that the principle is widely though not universally accepted.

How inter-confessional collaboration works in practice in the maritime ministry varies from port to port and with the differing temperaments, backgrounds and circumstances of the people involved, but certain common features can be observed. At a seafarers' centre operated ecumenically the members of the chaplaincy staff and the manager meet regularly to discuss the day to day running of the centre and formulate policy. Daily prayers are said together. The allocation of ships to be visited, and duties to be undertaken at the centre, is decided together. Specific tasks like hospital visiting, arranging transport for seafarers, the conduct of public worship, addressing meetings, and representing the centre at particular functions, are arranged by mutual consent. Regular times for reflection and discussion are an integral part of the programme. The importance of consultation and conveying information is accepted. It is a cardinal principle that every chaplain's loyalty to his particular ecclesiastical discipline and tradition is respected without question. The strength of the partnership lies in the loyalty of all concerned to their individual ecclesiastical tradition, to each other, to the whole team and to their common ministry.

The strengthening of inter-confessional collaboration has been another major concern of the International Christian Maritime Association, and the arrangement of regular regional and world-wide conferences of people involved in maritime ministry has greatly helped this. Such conferences are happy occasions. The participants learn more about each other's traditions and practices, friendships are made across denominational differences, and common worship leads to a deeper longing for intercommunion. Issues of common concern are discussed. Action on behalf of all can be agreed. Fellowship in the Gospel of Jesus Christ becomes increasingly more important. Solidarity with Christians of other denominations becomes a visible reality.

The Churches in the maritime world have come a long way in their quest for unity. But there is a long way still to go. Intercommunion between all Christians is not yet a reality. Some people have genuine reservations about inter-confessional collaboration. Some people are more adventurous than others. But a beginning has been made, and beginnings are important.

Notes

1. Quotation from a chaplain's reply to a questionnaire sent out by The Missions to Seamen to its staff in 1976. The findings were set out in a document entitled 'The Missions to Seamen in the Future' and circulated in 1977.
2. Ibid. Appendix A, p. 8.
3. Duncan Harris, Lay Warden of The Missions to Seamen, Port of Spain, Trinidad, 1985.
4. David Pellatt, Lay Chaplain of The Missions to Seamen in Bahrain, 1987.
5. 'Proclaiming the Gospel, or Caring is not Enough', a paper by The Revd. T. W. J. Ranson, 1984. This excellent paper was circulated in the General Secretary's Newsletter sent out by The Missions to Seamen in February 1985.
6. The Revd. Philip Thirlwell, The Missions to Seamen, Newcastle (New South Wales), 1985.

VI The Church's Ministry to Seafarers
Today (B)

International, Comprehensive, Prophetic, Flexible

International

'Let the peoples praise thee, O God; let all the peoples praise thee.'

Psalm 67, verse 5.

The spiritual, moral and material welfare of all seafarers, regardless of considerations of race, rank, religion, ideology or any other sort, is and always has been the primary concern of all the Christian organisations ministering to seafarers on an international basis except the Nordic seamen's missions, which because of their constitutions minister almost exclusively to Nordic seafarers and Nordic expatriate communities in their stations overseas.

When the Reformed Churches in Britain and the United States of America began to establish ministries to seamen and seamen's missions overseas in the nineteenth century, they sent missionaries from their own countries to pioneer the work. In the case of the British organisations—the British and Foreign Sailors' Society (as it then was) and The Missions to Seamen—they established themselves mainly but not exclusively where the British flag flew, English was spoken or there were sizeable communities of expatriate British people. They ministered to all seafarers, but it has to be remembered that at that time many seafarers spoke English anyway.

Between the middle of the nineteenth and the middle of the twentieth centuries the whole situation gradually changed. The British Empire declined. The United States of America, the Soviet Union and later China became increasingly powerful.

World trade increased phenomenally, and the merchant shipping fleets of a number of countries grew impressively. The
seamen's missions also changed. More and more they ministered to increasing numbers of seafarers from poorer countries
and non-Christian backgrounds: their culture was different,
their standards were different, and their languages were different. It became clear that in order to provide a ministry which
was relevant, appropriate and comprehensible it was now
necessary to appoint chaplaincy staff from a much wider range
of racial, cultural and linguistic backgrounds. In the years after
the Second World War centres specially designed to cater for
the particular needs of the large numbers of Asian seamen
visiting British ports were established. In the port of London
The Missions to Seamen opened a centre for West African
seafarers at Tilbury. In 1954 The Missions to Seamen
appointed a Chinese chaplain and set up a seafarers' centre
to minister to Chinese seafarers in London. The need was
recognised, but progress in meeting it was step by step and
slow.

The Anglican Church's ministry to seafarers is provided by
The Missions to Seamen. With the increasing autonomy of the
individual Provinces of the Anglican Communion and the
adoption of the principles of Mutual Responsibility and Inter-
Dependence and later Partnership in Mission, it was logical
and natural for The Missions to Seamen, as an integral part of
the Anglican Communion, to see its role no longer simply as a
missionary society of the Church of England but rather as the
international organisation of the Anglican Communion
ministering to the seafarers of the world. Its Headquarters
became its Central Office. Its role was to be more co-
ordinating and consultative than directing. National Councils
were established in many parts of the world. Liaison Bishops
were appointed by many Provinces to monitor the work of
maritime ministry within their jurisdiction and to keep in
touch with developments on the world scene through the
Central Office. Increasingly Diocesan Bishops have consulted
the Liaison Bishops and appointed Chaplains from their own
countries to maritime ministries within their dioceses. Now
The Missions to Seamen is fast becoming the international
organisation of the Anglican Communion ministering to
seafarers it saw it had to be.

The undenominational British Sailors' Society developed along the lines of linking up national associations with varying degrees of autonomy and directing the remainder from the London Headquarters. In Canada, South Africa and New Zealand the local associations manage their own affairs while retaining close links with London.

Among the organisations of the Lutheran Church ministering to seafarers the German Seamen's Mission has moved decisively into international and inter-confessional collaboration. In the 1970's a visionary outlook and great determination on the part of their General Secretary and Board members led to their taking or sharing the lead in establishing major seafarers' centres in Felixstowe and Jakarta. Both are run in partnership with other Christian organisations. Serious difficulties were encountered in the planning stages of both projects. But the difficulties were tackled and overcome, and the forging of a partnership with the Indonesian Communion of Churches in the ownership and operation of the Jakarta centre was a historic milestone. The Danish Seamen's Church moved into inter-confessional ministry in Hong Kong and Yokohama, working under one roof with the Apostleship of the Sea and The Missions to Seamen, though continuing to work mainly among Danish seafarers. Though the other Nordic seamen's missions continue to minister almost entirely to Nordic seafarers, their personnel are increasingly taking part in regional and plenary conferences held under the auspices of the International Christian Maritime Association.

When the Roman Catholic Church established the Apostleship of the Sea in 1921 it added an entirely new dimension to the whole realm of maritime ministry. Because the Apostleship of the Sea was the official arm of the Roman Catholic Church ministering to seafarers, the Diocesan Bishops appointed diocesan priests to serve as port chaplains, many of whom were indigenous to the dioceses where they served. Naturally as a body they represented a wide range of racial, national and cultural backgrounds, and the international conferences of the Apostleship of the Sea automatically had a far broader base than those of the missionary societies of the Reformed Churches. With the establishment of the Pontifical Commission for the Pastoral Care of Migrant and Itinerant People in 1970, the Apostleship of the Sea was linked with other apostolates to itinerant people, and a further dimension was added to the concept of maritime ministry.

This brief sketch of the development of an international outlook among the Christian organisations ministering to seafarers has been necessary because without this background it is difficult to understand maritime ministry today. The remainder of this section is concerned with illustrating the international nature of current maritime ministry.

Around the world a number of seafarers' centres have chaplaincy teams which are not only inter-confessional but also international in composition. At Dar es Salaam, in Tanzania, the Senior Chaplain is a Japanese Anglican Bishop, John Watanabe; he was Bishop of Hokkaido and Primate of the Nippon Sei Ko Kai (the Anglican Church of Japan) before resigning ten years before retirement in order to become a seafarers' chaplain. He was trained at The Missions to Seamen in Melbourne by a Chinese chaplain. The Roman Catholic chaplain is a French priest, Father Georges Loire of the White Fathers (the Society of Missionaries of Africa). The Warden/Manager is a Liverpool-born ex-seafarer Anglican Lay Reader, David Hodgson. Their staff meetings, which are conducted in English, are a triumph of communication! In Vancouver the Senior Chaplain is an Anglican priest from the South of Ireland, Joe Parker. Father Roland Joncas, the Roman Catholic chaplain, is the only member of the team who was born in Canada. Two Presbyterian ministers—Paul Tong, born in Taiwan, and I Shim Ro, born in Korea—complete the team. At the Seamen's Church Institute of New York and New Jersey, where the chaplaincy team is inter-confessional and international, a Korean Anglican Bishop, William Choi (formerly Bishop of Pusan), is currently under training. Like Bishop Watanabe, he resigned early in order to take up this ministry. In Tomakomai, in Japan, a new ministry to seafarers was established in 1986. The inspiration for it came from a young Japanese Anglican layman, Joseph Machida, and his parish priest Father Imagi, now Bishop of Hokkaido. The team is international and inter-confessional, and a striking feature of it is that every single church in the town is wholeheartedly involved in this ministry. The Roman Catholic Church made available a good building for use as a seafarers' centre, and it is called The Flying Angel Stella Maris Club. These are just four examples of international and inter-confessional chaplaincies. Many more could be cited.*

At the heart of all ministry is the gathering of the faithful around the Lord's Table. In this connection a celebration of Holy Communion in the chapel of the seafarers' centre in Vancouver in 1983 is vividly imprinted on the writer's memory. There were 28 seafarers present. They came from 18 countries. Two were from the People's Republic of China. The service was conducted in English. The Epistle was read and a three minute sermon given, in the Chinese dialect of the two Chinese seafarers, by Paul Tong, the Taiwanese-born Presbyterian minister. The Gospel and another three minute address were in English. The Lord's Prayer was said in 18 languages at once—and was quite chaotic! As far as possible each seafarer was given the Sacrament in a language he understood. It was a most moving service, and thoroughly international.

The ministry is international and inter-confessional.

Comprehensive

'I look upon all the world as my parish'
John Wesley, in his Journal, June 11 1739

Throughout the New Testament the Christian is constantly reminded that God's commission to His Church is to proclaim the Good News of Jesus Christ to all people, and on the maritime scene the Churches have realised that their ministry includes not only those who sail on ships but also those whose words, decisions and actions affect the lives and work of seafarers and their families. The Church's ministry in the maritime world is comprehensive, embracing all whose lives and work are in any way bound up with shipping and seafaring. A study of the many forms of maritime ministry which the Churches undertake indicates that they are beginning to achieve this aim, though much still remains to be done.

In ports all over the world, with the exception of certain countries under totalitarian regimes, the Churches provide an active positive ministry of welcome, care and Christian

* These four illustrations portray the scene as it was in mid 1988 when this section was written.

fellowship to merchant seafarers, naval personnel, fishermen, pilots, tug crews and those who serve on light vessels and in lighthouses. Christians engaged in full time lay or ordained ministry in docks and harbours frequently find themselves greeting and passing the time of day with officials from Customs, Immigration, Port Health and the Port Authority; they often find that when a problem arises their conversations suddenly assume a deeper significance, and the fact that they are regularly seen in the port and on the ships establishes a basis of trust. They also come into contact with shipping agents, ships' chandlers, trade union officials, dock workers and the many other people whose daily work is part of the life of a port. All these people can directly affect the lives and work of seafarers by their words and actions, and often the only contact some of them have with the Church is through Christians at work in the port and on the ships. The Church's ministry in the maritime world must embrace all who work in ports.

Maritime ministry extends beyond docks, harbours, ships and the people who work in and around them. Christian maritime organisations care for seafarers in hospital or prison. They provide chaplaincy services and sometimes seafarers' centres in sea training establishments. They provide retirement homes for ageing seafarers, family-style homes for the orphaned children of seafarers, and seafarers' medical centres. They organise seafarers' family support groups in seafaring communities. In Hong Kong The Missions to Seamen and the Apostleship of the Sea operate a Family Services department as part of the outreach of the Mariners' Clubs; fully trained Chinese Christian social workers provide a wide range of services in the local seafaring community.

The Church's ministry in the maritime world embraces also the people at the highest level whose deliberations, decisions and actions directly affect the lives of seafarers and others involved in shipping. Shipowners, government officials, officers of organisations like the International Maritime Organisation, the International Labour Organisation, the International Shipping Federation and the International Transport Workers Federation, national seamen's welfare boards and directors of crew recruiting agencies, are all involved in the decision-making processes. In certain countries and ports individual Christian organisations enjoy well-established relations with some of these influential people. On the international scene the formation of the International Christian Maritime Association has led to the establishment of important links with the International Maritime Organisation, the International Labour Organisation, the International Shipping Federation, the International Transport Workers Federation and the International Council of Seamen's Welfare. Strenuous efforts are being made to develop these links further. Many corporate and individual links between the Churches and the decision makers have been forged. The Church's voice is heard and listened to in the maritime world.

In assessing how far the Churches provide a comprehensive ministry in the maritime world it is necessary to identify both what has already been achieved and also what will need to be done in the future.

The achievements already described give some indication of the wide range of activities in which the individual organisations, and more recently the International Christian Maritime Association, have been involved. They are like the individual pieces of a jigsaw puzzle which make a whole picture only when all the pieces are joined together. What has happened is that the coming together of all the different organisations in free association in the International Christian Maritime Association has opened up exciting new areas of rationalisation, collaboration and joint action which have still to be developed. Time is needed to think through all the implications and gather the necessary resources. Enormous progress has been made. Goodwill among the hierarchies of the Christian organisations ministering to seafarers is a fact. Much rationalisation has taken place. Christians of different denominations work happily together under one roof as partners in ministry, and the strength of their ministry together has been enhanced. New joint work has been established in many ports. The impact of their concerted voice and action is felt on the whole shipping scene. The contribution of the International Christian Maritime Association has been in the organisation of regular plenary and regional conferences, the promotion of joint action between the individual organisations, and its publications which tell the seafarer what the Churches are doing together.

In the future, serious consideration will need to be given to a number of important issues if the maritime ministry of the Churches is to become more comprehensive. The Churches need representation at an appropriate level on important official bodies making decisions affecting the lives of seafarers. They need a more united and comprehensive approach to seafarers, difficult though that may be for national, geographical and other reasons. They need to consider the whole question of providing ministry to all people on the move, like airline crews, international road transport personnel and people moving regularly from one place or country to another. They need to make the Church as a whole more aware of what they have achieved already in interconfessional and comprehensive ministry. They need to analyse and further develop their contacts and relationships with people of other faiths.

The Church's ministry to seafarers has already attained a measure of comprehensiveness. It is becoming more comprehensive. It will be fully comprehensive when the whole shipping world hears the Word of God.

Prophetic

'Then I heard the Lord saying, Whom shall I send?
Who will go for me? And I answered, Here am I;
Send me. He said, Go and tell this people . . .'

Isaiah, Chapter 6, verses 8 and 9.

It is a basic tenet of Christianity that all people are made in the image of God and are of equal value and importance to Him. As equals, therefore, they should treat each other with justice, dignity and respect. But from the beginning of history some nations, groups of people and individuals have sought to exploit other nations, groups of people and individuals.

In every age there have been servants of God who stood out against the injustice, oppression, extortion, greed and self-centredness which accompany such an attitude. With great determination Moses led the Israelites out of slavery and humiliation in Egypt. With great courage the prophets of Israel denounced injustice, oppression and greed wherever and whenever they encountered it.

When Jesus Christ came into the world He proclaimed that His followers should not only love God with their whole being but also their neighbours as themselves. He died for His teachings. But He was raised from death. The power of evil could not overcome Him. The presence of evil could not invalidate what He taught. He lives in His Church today.

Throughout the 1900 years of its life the history of the Church is adorned with many examples of servants of God who courageously opposed injustice, violence, and the abuse of the dignity and value of people. Few were popular with the recipients of their message. Some gave their lives in the process.

Declaring God's word for a particular situation at a particular time is the essence of prophecy.

In the maritime world the Churches and Christian organisations have been active in combating injustice, oppression, greed and vice wherever it has appeared, and they have often been roundly abused for their pains.

In the nineteenth century seafarers' chaplains fought (physically sometimes) for the stamping out of the evil practice of crimping.* They campaigned for improved conditions for seafarers on board ship, for the introduction of officially recognised leisure time for seafarers on ships at sea on Sundays, and for the provision of good leisure facilities ashore for seafarers as an attractive alternative to dockside gin palaces, taverns and brothels. Their campaigns were effective. Crimping was eradicated, conditions on ships improved enormously, leisure time at sea on Sundays became standard on ships of many countries, and seafarers' centres were established in many ports of the world.

But as fast as one set of abuses was stamped out, another appeared. As times change, so do abuses. They do not totally disappear, they surface again in different guises. In the 1980's there are a number of thoroughly evil situations in the maritime world to which the Churches and Christian organisations are drawing attention and on which they are taking action.

With the current chronic surplus of ships, a deep and long lasting worldwide trade recession, keen competition for the

* See Chapters One, Two and Three, pages 3–61.

cargoes that are available, and the opportunity to purchase second-hand ships reasonably cheaply, a small but very active class of ship operators has come into being whose business ethics and methods fall far short of acceptable standards. They usually operate under the flag of a country whose safety regulations are neither stringent nor rigorously enforced and whose taxes are light. Often the ships are inadequately maintained. Crews are recruited through national or international manning agencies in countries where wages are low, unemployment is high, and people are desperate for work of any kind at almost any rate of pay. International pay guidelines are ignored or flouted. Often a ship leaves port with bills unpaid, and when the creditors begin to press hard for payment the name of the ship and the port of registration are changed, the owner adopts a low profile, and the whole dishonest charade continues. The people who suffer most are the seafarers who man such ships. Often they are not paid for many months, and so cannot leave the ship. They know that if they complain they may be dismissed and reported to the manning agency or the appropriate government office in their home country; they may then be blacklisted, and never get another job at sea. Sometimes the ship is arrested in port for non-payment of accounts in other ports, or for unseaworthiness; then the seafarers may be stranded for months without money, fuel or food. Such ships are not uncommon—three examples were quoted in Chapter Four. The problem is a significant one, the more so since it undermines the efforts of the large majority of good shipowners and trade unions.

Seafarers on such ships turn naturally to seafarers' chaplains for help, since they visit ships and can see for themselves the truth or otherwise of some of the complaints, and are known to be caring people and part of the worldwide Church. One example, from Sarnia in Canada, of how the Church as a whole can help vividly illustrates the point.

'Duncan Harris, Warden of The Missions to Seamen in Port of Spain, Trinidad, notified the chaplain in Toronto (Fr. Mulholland) by phone and mail that the "Prometheus V" would be coming to Canada in December 1985. The crew had not been paid for nearly a year, and was owed some U.S. $24,500. This was not the only problem, for on Christmas Day, 1984, Mr. Harris had to take the crew ashore and feed them because there were only rotten eggs on board. The ship had sailed for Canada with some equipment and safety devices not functioning properly.

'The ship was owned by the Admiralty International Shipping Company and registered in Panama; the company was owned by a Greek resident of New York City. Mr. Julio Chanson, of the Panamanian Maritime Directory in New York, was monitoring the ship for the many infractions of the Panamanian code which could rescind Panamanian registration of the ship.

'The vessel was due to call in Sarnia, Ontario, to pick up a cargo of beans destined for the Nicaraguan port of Corinto, so Fr. Mulholland, of the Missions to Seamen in Toronto, notified Mr. Herbert Jackson, lay Chaplain of their station in Sarnia, of its imminent arrival, and provided him with the names of those in the Spanish-speaking crew who spoke English.

'The "Prometheus V" arrived in Sarnia on December 9th, but was not allowed to berth until dockage fees were paid. On December 10th. Mr. Jackson contacted the Roman Catholic parish priest, Fr. Emil Donanzen, chaplain of the Apostleship of the Sea, and they agreed to go aboard the ship together as soon as it berthed. They went on board on December 11th.

'A distraught crew fell upon them when they came up the ship's ladder, all saying "Please help us", and that they had not been paid for eleven months. The condition of the ship was deplorable. Florenzo Legato, the second cook, came up to them in a pitiable state. He dropped his trousers to show the two chaplains a large lumpy growth in his lower abdomen, explaining that he could no longer lift things. The captain, a Burmese, had told him that he could not go ashore for medical attention because there was no money to pay for it. He was obviously in need of urgent attention.

'Deeply disturbed by what they had seen and heard, Mr. Jackson and Fr. Donanzen then met with the ship's protective agent in Sarnia, Jack Brown. (Mr. Brown is a member of the Board of The Missions to Seamen in Sarnia.) It was agreed that it was likely that the crew would go on strike unless some money was advanced, and this was put by phone to the agents in Montreal. Because of the conditions on board calls were made to Mr. Julio Chanson at the Maritime Directory. After the agents had contacted the owners it was agreed that $10,000 would be sent immediately to pay port dues, an advance of wages, and agency fees. On being informed of developments, The Missions to Seamen in Toronto phoned Mr. Andrew Boyle, Executive Vice-President of the Seafarers' International Union of Canada and representative of the International Transport Workers Federation, to apprise him of the horrible situation and the approximate date of the ship's arrival in Montreal.

'That evening Fr. Donanzen took the Burmese captain to dinner with a family of his compatriots in Sarnia, while Herb Jackson returned to the ship in The Missions to Seamen mobile club (donated by the International Transport Workers Federation). He ascertained that some money had been given to the crew who wished to go shopping. He took eleven crew members, who were not on duty (because the ship was already loading beans), in the mobile club to a local shopping centre. Nearly all of these men bought suitcases, which led Herb to believe that if they were not paid they would jump ship. The men were driven back to the ship at 2230 hours.

'The next day, 12th December, Herb Jackson again went to the ship to take the remainder of the crew shopping. While waiting for the seamen to get into the mobile club, the ship's captain asked him to take the second cook, Florenzo Legato, to the doctor. Herb took him to the emergency department of St. Joseph's Hospital. After a lengthy examination the doctors there explained that Mr. Legato had a very serious double hernia, and that he should have immediate surgery. On being informed the captain said that he would arrange for him to be flown home from Montreal. Herb Jackson then took the remaining members of the crew shopping and gave them a tour of the city.

'On returning to the ship the entire crew came down on to the dock and presented Herb Jackson with a hand-carved Spanish galleon as a token for all The Missions to Seamen had done for them in Sarnia. Later that day the ship sailed for Montreal. Its progress was monitored through the Seaway.

'The "Prometheus V" arrived in Montreal on the 14th December. Andy Boyle for the I.T.F. went aboard to assess the situation. As a result of his efforts the crew received 80% of their outstanding wages (approximately U.S. $20,000). The second cook with the double hernia was repatriated to the Dominican Republic, with 100% of his wages in cash and the air ticket paid for. Mr. Boyle discovered that the vessel would be calling at a United States port in Louisiana and advised the crew to contact the local I.T.F. affiliate there if by then they had not received in cash the 20% of their wages still owing (approximately $4,500).

'The Canadian Coast Guard, alerted to the conditions of the ship, undertook a thorough safety inspection which cost the company tens of thousands of dollars. The ship was allowed to sail on December 23rd 1985.

'That this whole sorry business came to a happy conclusion is due to the network of Missions to Seamen stations who have followed the movements of this vessel for some thirteen months, and were able to alert the shipping agents, the Seafarers International Union of Canada, Canada Coastguard, and others, before the vessel arrived in their ports. This happy co-operation of Canadian business, union, inter-confessional chaplaincy and government in coming to the assistance of these badly used seamen living in deplorable and unsafe conditions is commendable'[1].

This is one example taken from one of a number of thick files containing similar reports from other ports. However, it is important to retain a sense of proportion. As has already been stated, such ships represent a small minority of the total number of ships at sea. But they represent an important minority, and the Church cannot be satisfied until such vessels no longer sail the oceans of the world.

In 1980 the Seamen's Church Institute of New York and New Jersey established the Center for Seafarers' Rights to handle the large and growing number of cases of injustice, exploitation and sub-human treatment of seafarers which were being reported in North America. The Revd. Dr. Paul Chapman, a Baptist minister who had been associated with The (late) Revd. Martin Luther King, was appointed to take charge of the Center's work, and his ministry developed rapidly and extensively. Working with co-operation from government offices, consulates, trade unions, shipowners, seafarers' welfare organisations, Christian missions to seafarers, the International Christian Maritime Association, the International Transport

Workers Federation and many other bodies, his team has produced advisory booklets for seafarers serving on ships of the major flag of convenience registries, and has organised conferences of interested parties on subjects such as the conditions of service of crew members on the cruise ships operating from North American ports, the establishment of a Code of Good Practices for Manning Agents, and Port State Control. Paul has travelled widely to speak to seafarers' chaplains about the work of the Center for Seafarers' Rights, and receives co-operation from many parts of the world. The operators of sub-standard ships have reason to take very seriously the prophetic ministry of the church.

In 1986 the Anglican Missions to Seamen appointed a senior member of staff to correlate information and monitor action in cases of injustice to seafarers. He works closely with the Center for Seafarers' Rights, the International Christian Maritime Association and other Christian and secular organisations. The International Transport Workers Federation is able to give considerable assistance in most cases.

In 1987 the Roman Catholic Apostleship of the Sea ended its eighteenth World Congress with a 'Message to Seafarers'. Part of it was as follows:

'Assembled in Mombasa, Kenya, for the XVIII World Congress of the Apostleship of the Sea, we, Cardinals, Bishops, priests, deacons, religious, seafarers, fishermen, their families and other people committed to their cause, feel involved in every aspect of maritime life, both spiritual and temporal, and concerned with the changes that are affecting it today.

We have shared our experience of maritime life in both industrialised and third world countries . . .

We have reaffirmed the extent to which human dignity is defiled on numerous occasions in the seafarer's daily life:
— in the way he is recruited,
— in his working conditions
— in the lack of social security
— in increasing unemployment

All such circumstances are patently unacceptable, since they often lead to new forms of slavery . . .'

The Roman Catholic Church pulls no punches in its prophetic ministry.

Increasingly the International Christian Maritime Association, as the free association of the major Christian organisations ministering to seafarers, voices their common view on major matters. In 1985 the resolutions of its Plenary Conference, which was held in the Philippines and considered inter alia some of the problems experienced by Filipino seafarers, were conveyed personally to the Government of the Philippines by the Head of the Roman Catholic Church there, Cardinal Jaime Sin. In 1987 it organised a conference in Manila to discuss the problems of manning agencies in the Philippines. It has issued approved statements on major issues such as the dangers facing seafarers on ships entering the waters of the Arabian/Persian Gulf. Its regional conferences regularly discuss such matters.

The Church's ministry to seafarers in the 1980's is prophetic.

Flexible

'His mother said to the servants, "Do whatever he tells you."'

St. John, chapter 5, verse 2.

If maritime ministry is to be relevant and appropriate it must be flexible.

The shipping world is constantly changing and developing. Patterns of trade change. Ports rise and decline in importance. Ships spend varying lengths of time in port, depending on the cargo they are handling, and berth at varying distances from the nearest centre of population. Many ships' crews are multinational, multi-cultural, multi-faith and multi-lingual in composition. Political factors may determine whether or not seafarers come ashore to relax. Climatic conditions may decide how they spend their shore leave.

The Church must constantly monitor the changes in the shipping scene if it is to fulfil its ministry effectively. As well as taking note of developments in the industry it must also work out their implications. It must ask questions like these: is full-time or part-time ministry required? does the ministry require the services of an ordained priest or minister? if so, on what basis? is there a need for a seafarers' centre? how can the local parishes and congregations be involved in the ministry? what are the priorities in a particular port?

The nature of contemporary maritime ministry is encouragingly flexible.

There is a deep and growing appreciation in the Churches that this ministry should be a partnership between clergy, laity, local congregations, the Church as a whole, the shipping industry locally, nationally and internationally, and all whose actions affect the lives of seafarers. There is a clear realisation of the importance of making the best and fullest use of clergy and laity alike—in a number of busy ports the shipboard ministry, administration and daily running of a seafarers' centre is the responsibility of well-qualified and able lay people who can call on the services of part-time or honorary chaplains whenever appropriate, while in others an ordained person in charge is more suitable.

There is flexibility in the facilities the Churches currently provide for seafarers. Around the ports of the world most of the old 'Seamen's Institutes', which were notable for their vastness, austerity and somewhat impersonal character, have disappeared and been replaced by smaller, brighter, well-equipped, easily-managed and sometimes relocatable centres. In some short-stay spread-out ports, like Halifax in Nova Scotia, Sarnia and Toronto in the Great Lakes of Canada, and Great Yarmouth and Aberdeen in the United Kingdom, mobile centres have been introduced; comfortably fitted-out and well-equipped with telephones, shop, book store, and a host of other amenities, these large motor vehicles move from remote berth to remote berth as required, meeting a real need. Some chaplains carry out their ministry from their specially-adapted homes, to which they invite seafarers. The Nordic seafarers' societies operate from Scandinavian-style homes in which the members of staff have their own private quarters. And a number of seafarers' chaplains work without the back-up of any kind of seafarers' centre at all.

There is flexibility, too, in the Churches' services to seafarers. The provision of transport for seafarers to and from the seafarers' centre and for sporting activities and tours, a worldwide network of support for the seafarer with a problem, information on a host of subjects, arranging interpreters for seafarers in hospital or detention, counselling for those who need it, and just being available, are some of the many ways in which they can and do help at any time.

But it is supremely in person-to-person contact with seafarers that maritime ministry demonstrates its flexibility. Being sensitive to differences of race, rank, religion, culture or ideology, offering a service without giving the impression of being patronising, and respecting other people's beliefs and being prepared to discuss them without prejudice are all hallmarks of those engaged in this work. So are being prepared to conduct acts of worship of various kinds on board ship or in the chapel at any hour of the day or night, among people some of whom may not understand the language being used, hearing a seafarer's confession at any time, and allaying superstitious fears.

A seafarers' chaplain seldom knows what any day is likely to hold in store for him. He goes where His Lord leads, and tries to do what He says.

Notes

1. Report from The Revd. J. D. Mulholland, chaplain of the Missions to Seamen, Toronto.

VII The International Christian Maritime Association

'The glory which thou gavest me I have given to them, that they may be one as we are one: I in them and thou in me, may they be perfectly one. Then the world will know that thou didst send me, that thou didst love them as thou didst me.'

St. John, chapter 17, verses 22 and 23.

There can be no doubt that the most significant event of the last quarter of a century in the sphere of maritime ministry was the establishment of the International Christian Maritime Association.

Before it came into being the individual Christian denominational and undenominational organisations generally (but with honourable exceptions) operated independently and often gave the impression of being in competition with each other. It has already been noted (Chapter 2 p. 25) that the two major British-based organisations ministering internationally to seafarers before the First World War, the British and Foreign Sailors' Society and The Missions to Seamen, were seldom in communication, though much of their work was similar and could have benefited from a sharing of ideas and resources. When the Roman Catholic Church established the Apostleship of the Sea after the First World War, and quickly developed a world-wide network of chaplaincies and seafarers' centres, it seemed to many non-Roman Catholics that another distinct and competitive element had appeared on the scene. The Nordic seamen's missions, from their foundation in the second half of the nineteenth century, actively pursued their policy of ministering almost exclusively to Nordic seafarers and Nordic expatriate communities, and their work scarcely impinged upon the organisations operating internationally. Until well after the Second World War there was little meaningful contact between the chaplains, lay staff and voluntary workers of the various organisations, and suspicion of each other's activities and motives were regrettably common. The attitudes of the different organisations involved in maritime ministry reflected many of the attitudes prevailing in the Churches at that time.

After the Second World War a slow but perceptible change in inter-Church relations began to gather momentum. The traumas of two World Wars had united Christians of all denominations in practical pastoral ministry in emergency situations, and a number of barriers had been undermined. In the Reformed Churches there was a growing determination to promote reunification schemes, and the inauguration in 1947 of the Church of South India, which brought together Anglicans, Congregationalists, Presbyterians and Methodists, was a significant landmark. In 1948 the World Council of Churches was formally constituted: it included all the major denominations of the Western Church (except the Roman Catholic and the Unitarian Churches), most of the Eastern Orthodox Churches, and many Asian and African Churches: in 1961 the Roman Catholic Church established a link with it by appointing accredited observers to its Assemblies. In the 1950's the Annual Week of Prayer for Christian Unity in which most major denominations now participate began to be observed more widely in many countries. In 1958 Cardinal Angelo Roncalli was elected Pope John XXIII, and in a little over four years he changed the face of Christendom. He brought to his task a transparent love of people and the Church, a willingness and determination to break down barriers of prejudice and insularity, and a longing for the ultimate unity of all Christian people. In 1960 the Anglican Archbishop of Canterbury Geoffrey Fisher paid a historic visit to Pope John XXIII in Rome and commented on his return that the Church of Rome was no longer an enemy but an ally. At every level in the Western Church there was a crumbling of long-established barriers and a growing perception of what unity might mean.

In the maritime ministry the separateness of the Churches was reflected in the independent operations of the individual organisations, the proliferation of seafarers' centres in some ports, the duplication of effort in many, and the mutual suspicion which existed between chaplains, lay staff and volunteers of the different denominations. But as the Churches moved tentatively towards inter-confessional collaboration a number of people engaged in maritime ministry glimpsed a vision of what this could mean in their particular work.

In 1951 the National Council of Seamen's Agencies* (which in 1967 changed its name to the International Council of Seamen's Agencies) was established in North America to bring together Christian and other organisations involved in serving seafarers. Its aim was to 'engage in such Christian activities of a philanthropic literary and educational nature as promote and develop the spiritual, moral and physical welfare of seamen ashore and afloat'.[1] In 1968 the British Sailors' Society and The Missions to Seamen set up the Seafarers' Trust to be the 'clearing house' for operations they proposed to establish and operate jointly; by the mid 1960's they were already working in partnership in Par in Cornwall and Fremantle in Western Australia and had plans for further collaboration. In 1967, when The Missions to Seamen held a 'world conference' in Oxford for members of its staff and voluntary workers, official visitors included Monsignor Francis Frayne from the Apostleship of the Sea in Rome (who was later to become one of the Secretaries of the Pontifical Commission for the Pastoral Care of Migrant and Itinerant People set up by Pope Paul VI in 1970), and Archbishop Emmanuele Clarizio (later to become Pro-President of the Pontifical Commission). On both sides of the Atlantic some positive actions had been taken in the Reformed Churches to initiate inter-Society collaboration, and the Second Vatican Council had committed the Roman Catholic Church to the path of inter-confessional collaboration.

In 1966 the National Council of Seamen's Agencies in North America made a decision at its Annual General Meeting to organise an international consultation in Europe to discuss the provision of services to seafarers with as wide a range as possible of people from all over the world with experience in this work. Contact was established with the World Council of Churches in 1967 and in December 1968, after long and careful preparation, the International (as it had become) Council of Seamen's Agencies and the Division of World Mission and Evangelism of the World Council of Churches extended an invitation to interested people and organisations

---

* See page 50 for the background of this organisation.

to take part in an International Consultation on Services to Seafarers to be held in Rotterdam in August 1969. In March 1969 the Apostleship of the Sea, the British Sailors' Society and The Missions to Seamen became joint sponsors of the Consultation together with the Nederlandse Zeemanscentrale, the Nordic Missions to Seamen and the two inviting organisations. An organising committee was set up in Rotterdam, and its chairman was a pastor of the Nederlandse Zeemanscentrale, The Revd. Jacob Schokking.

More than a hundred delegates from 52 national and international voluntary Christian organisations attended this first-ever world-wide, inter-confessional Consultation on Services to Seafarers.

They came from a wide variety of backgrounds. Monsignor Francis Frayne, from the office of the Apostleship of the Sea in Rome, and Father Alphonse Laureys from Antwerp, were among a number of Roman Catholics present. The Revd. Tom Kerfoot, General Secretary, was one of the representatives of The (Anglican) Missions to Seamen. The Revd. Johannes Aardal, General Secretary of the Norwegian Seamen's Mission, and The Revd. Palle Neilsen, General Secretary of the Danish Seamen's Church in Foreign Ports, were among the representatives of the Lutheran Churches in Northern Europe. From the International Council of Seamen's Agencies in North America came many outstanding people, including The Revd. Bernard Spong, a Lutheran Chaplain from New York and President of the Council at the time the decision was taken to arrange the Consultation, Dr. Emile Dieth, from New Orleans, Chairman of the Consultation's Steering Committee, The Revd. Dr. John Mulligan, Director of the Seamen's Church Institute of New York, The Revd. Hans Uittenbosch from Montreal, The Revd. Arthur Bartlett of the Seamen's Church Institute of San Pedro, Canon Stanley Smith of The Missions to Seamen in Vancouver, and The Revd. Joseph Abbott of The Missions to Seamen in Toronto. Commander John Hough, General Secretary, was one of the representatives of the un-denominational British Sailors' Society. Leslie Hartley, of the Sailors' Children's Society in Hull, Moshe Pomrock, of the Israel Maritime League, and The Revd. Geoffrey Sturman, an Anglican Industrial Chaplain, represented widely different interests. The Revd. Dr. Daisuko Kitagawa. Secretary for

Urban and Industrial Mission in the Department of World Mission and Evangelism, represented the World Council of Churches. Dr. Enrico Argiroffo represented the International Labour Office. The port and municipality of Rotterdam were represented by the Burgomaster and Mr. C. Grundel, Director of the Seamen's Welfare Office. Captain Wim Kuijper, a Master Mariner and Chairman of the Netherlands Christian Seafarers' Society, and Mr. A. Bouman, of the Amsterdam Hospital Church ship 'de Hoop', were among other Dutch representatives. There were many other knowledgeable, experienced and distinguished people present, but sadly they are too numerous to name individually.

They came from a wide age range. One of the youngest was The Revd. Brian Simmons, a Master Mariner and chaplain of The Missions to Seamen at the National Pre-Sea Training School at Gravesend in England. There were chaplains and lay workers in the middle years of their ministry, and there were wise and outstanding chaplains and leaders with years of experience behind them as they approached the end of their full-time ministry.

Most were strong personalities. Many were people accustomed to being ultimately responsible for their own and other people's work and to taking important decisions. Many had been involved in their particular tradition and area of maritime ministry for a long time. They were not the sort of people who could be pushed around.

The aims of the Consultation were straightforward. They were:

(i) to acquire a knowledge of the particular circumstances and problems of seafaring today,
(ii) to examine to what extent these problems are being solved by the present work of Agencies and Organisations throughout the world,
(iii) to assess what more is required, and
(iv) to agree upon and formulate appropriate action to be taken at local, national and international level.

A questionnaire relevant to the purpose of the Consultation had been circulated to intending participants, and their replies had been carefully analysed and correlated.

What happened at the Consultation was manifestly the work of the Holy Spirit.

It opened with a combined act of worship in St. Laurens Church, and that in itself was a new experience for many of the delegates. The order of service was printed in Dutch, and the hymns were translated into other languages. The first of the two addresses was given by Pastor Jacob Schokking, Chairman of the Organising Committee. He based what he said on the 13th verse of the 13th chapter of St. Paul's First Letter to the Corinthians: 'There are three things that last for ever: faith, hope and love; but the greatest of them all is love.' He spoke of the need to put away fears of change and to concentrate on what is eternal. In this way they could look ahead to a great future. 'That is why we are here together . . . representing many countries and cultures, members of different church formations with various traditions, customs and hymns. This is no easy or superficial ecumenism . . . We are here together because faith and hope remain active, because . . . we are moving with His great strides towards His future, inspired by His Spirit, guided by His compassion.'[2] The service set the tone for the whole gathering.

The Consultation was guided by some outstanding introductory addresses. The opening speech was made by the Chairman of the Steering Committee, Dr. Emile Dieth, who spoke about how the Consultation had originated, of its aims, and how it was the work of Christian optimists. Monsignor Frayne gave a lucid and concise paper on 'The Seafarer as a Person and the World in which he lives', and Captain Kuijper spoke on the same subject from a seafarer's point of view. The Revd. Brian Simmons spoke of his current ministry among boys preparing for life at sea at the biggest sea-training school in the world. Dr. Argiroffo gave a clear and comprehensive picture of the maritime work of the International Labour Office, Mr. J. W. Hupkes, Managing Director of the Rhine-Schelde Group, spoke about the latest developments in the shipping industry, The Honorable Barbara Watson, from the State Department, addressed the delegates on 'The Seafarer as an international citizen and the United States consul', and Dr. Daisuko Kitagawa, from the World Council of Churches, spoke about 'Seafarers as an International Community'.

Lively discussions took place in the workshops and in

informal meetings between plenary sessions. 'The emotions most strongly felt were surprise and amazement that such being together, working, organising, speaking, listening and praying together were possible. It is hard to realise now how separate we had been until then. There had also been not only the division of being in one's own world, but the others were often considered as rivals . . .'[3] A growing sense of excitement and expectation that something momentous would result from the meeting gripped those present. 'Most of us had the strong impression that God Himself was moving us forward, and away from our own small circles.'[4]

A number of important influences emerged. Monsignor Francis Frayne and The Revd. Tom Kerfoot, firm friends and men of charisma, intelligence and the ability to put visionary thoughts into practical terms and simple language were outstanding. The Revd. Johannes Aardal was a decisive influence among his Nordic colleagues. Dr. Daisuko Kitagawa 'was a personality all by himself, a real godly man'.[5] But the conference was not about individuals: it was about a common purpose. 'We were different, with different purposes, different motivations. But this we had in common: we were all concerned about seafarers.'[6]

Towards the end of the Consultation Tom Kerfoot led the delegates in a discussion about how their common purposes and new-found fellowship might best be advanced. Following this a comprehensive and admirably written six page document, entitled 'Conclusions and Resolutions as agreed in plenary session at Visser't Hooft Huis, Oostmaaslaan 80, Rotterdam, Netherlands' was prepared, the resolutions having been unanimously accepted. The Consultation agreed that:

(i) there was a 'need for an international association of Christian voluntary organisations to achieve collaboration in the furtherance of their common aims, and to serve as a means of more effective communication with other agencies'.

(ii) a committee should be set up 'to study the manner in which a permanent association of Christian voluntary agencies . . . may best be brought into being'.

(iii) the nature of such an association would be that of 'a consultative and representative body'.

(iv) the purpose of the association would be:
  (a) 'to foster collaboration and mutual aid among constituent bodies and to further common interests', and
  (b) 'to be the collective and respected voice of the association within the industry and outside it; which can offer counsel and be heard within the councils of those bodies whose deliberations in any way affect or influence the lives and welfare of seafarers'.

 (v) a working committee should be appointed to 'promote the implementation of the resolutions issuing from the Rotterdam Consultation', and

(vi) another international consultation should be called for 1972.

A truly memorable consultation ended with the spontaneous singing of the doxology 'Praise God from whom all blessings flow . . .' The International Christian Maritime Association (I.C.M.A.) had been born.

As often happens with conferences which make decisions with far-reaching implications, there were many practical matters which required urgent attention if the initial momentum was not to be lost.

The Working Committee, conscious of this, tackled its tasks with speed and efficiency. The Revd. Tom Kerfoot and Monsignor Francis Frayne were appointed joint chairmen, and the World Council of Churches generously made available the services first of Daisuko Kitagawa and then, after his death, Captain Jan Ørner, as Secretary, and allowed I.C.M.A. to have an official address at its offices in Geneva. Each member of the committee undertook a particular field of study relating to the development and interests of I.C.M.A., and this ensured that responsibility for its promotion did not fall on the shoulders of just one or two busy people. Work began on the preparation of a world directory of seafarers' agencies and centres, which would be published under the auspices of I.C.M.A. and made available through its member organisations to seafarers and the shipping industry. A draft Constitution was drawn up and circulated for comment and possible amendment, questions relating to international and inter-confessional collaboration were posed, current issues of life at sea and their implications for the Churches were examined, finance was considered, and an agenda for the 1972 international consultation, which would be held in London, was prepared. In 1970 I.C.M.A. was granted observer status at the Maritime Session of the International Labour Conference held in Geneva. Most important of all, the spirit of goodwill, friendship, fellowship and collaboration, which had sprung into life in Rotterdam, grew steadily stronger and deeper. Mutual confidence was being established.

The international consultation held in London in 1972 was the first plenary conference of I.C.M.A. It was attended by 185 participants, of whom 165 were delegates from 42 Christian organisations and the remainder guests or the observers from 8 secular maritime organisations. The list of principal guests was most impressive. It included The Revd. Dr. Eugene Carson Blake (General Secretary of the World Council of Churches), Archbishop Emmanuele Clarizio (Pro-President of the Pontifical Commission for the Pastoral Care of Migrants and Itinerant Peoples), Bishop John Howe (Secretary General of the Anglican Consultative Council), The Revd. G. A. D. Mann (General Secretary of the Free Church Federal Council), The Revd. Dr. J. Fraser McLuskey (representing the Moderator of the Church of Scotland), Bishop K. Sansbury (General Secretary of the British Council of Churches), Bishop B. C. Butler (representing Cardinal Heenan), and official delegates of the Lutheran Federation.

On the business side the conference adopted both the reports of the Working Committee, which had been set up in Rotterdam, and also the Constitution, copies of which had been sent out in advance. Various provisions of the Constitution are noteworthy. It stated that I.C.M.A. was 'a free association of Christian organisations engaged in welfare work for seafarers'. Plenary conferences would be held every three years. Its Standing Committee's function would be 'to carry out the general policy of I.C.M.A. as formulated in Conference from time to time and subject to any conditions imposed by Conference to provide for the administration, management and control of the affairs of I.C.M.A.'. The members of the Standing Committee were to comprise 'one representative from and appointed by each of the following:

'The Apostleship of the Sea, the German Seamen's Missions, the Nederlandse Zeemanscentrale, the Council of the Nordic Seamen's Missions (representing Seamen's Mission organisations in Denmark, Finland, Norway and Sweden), the International Council of Seamen's Agencies (Association of North and South American organisations), the Seafarers' Trust (The Missions to Seamen and British Sailors' Society), and the World Council of Churches.'

The membership clause was amended in 1975 to allow individual representation to The Missions to Seamen and the British Sailors' Society, and again in 1981 when the membership of the World Council of Churches ceased. Thus I.C.M.A. was formally constituted.

The conference then concentrated on aspects of maritime ministry. The major topics studied included the care of seafarers' families, ethnic and religious groups and their special needs, leaders and 'animators' on board ship, finance and the well-being of the seafarer (the financing of seafarers' facilities), and maritime training (related to the work of Christian seafarers' welfare organisations). In the resolutions adopted by the conference it is significant that delegates were concerned about seafarers' contractual agreements and the 'exploitive conditions of life and work experienced by some seafarers sailing under flags of convenience.'[7] As noted elsewhere in this book, these problems continue to cause concern in the late 1980's.

Between the plenary conferences in London in 1972 and Elsinore in 1975 the affairs of I.C.M.A. were handled by the Standing Committee. The Co-Chairmen were Prebendary Tom Kerfoot, of The Missions to Seamen, and The Revd. Johannes Aardal, of the Nordic Seamen's Missions Council, and the individual members continued to undertake specific assignments and tasks. But I.C.M.A. was developing fast, and the task of guiding and promoting its growth, expansion and increasing influence required more than the limited time and energy busy people in responsible positions within their own organisations could give. The need for a proper secretariat was becoming increasingly apparent.

This situation was resolved at the second plenary conference of I.C.M.A., which was held at Elsinore in Denmark in 1975. It was known in advance that Prebendary Tom Kerfoot was due to retire as General Secretary of The Missions to Seamen at the end of that year, and that he was ready, willing and eager to devote his time, energy, knowledge and extensive experience of maritime ministry to furthering the work of I.C.M.A. in his early retirement years. He was the obvious person to be its first General Secretary. Blessed with an attractive shyness of manner, he had great personal charm. He was in good health, had abundant energy, a phenomenal memory, and a deep longing for the unity of the Church. He had been one of the moving spirits in the establishment of I.C.M.A. six years previously. When he was invited to become General Secretary at a plenary session of the conference his acceptance was greeted with a standing ovation. The conference requested the Standing Committee to work out the details and financial implications of the appointment, and agreed that I.C.M.A. should be responsible for financing the secretariat. The manner in which the logistics of the appointment were handled was typical of the spirit which permeated the activities of I.C.M.A. The Missions to Seamen made available, free of charge, an office, some secretarial assistance and the use of its office equipment, the Apostleship of the Sea financed the cost of raising Prebendary Kerfoot's pension income to an appropriate level and contributed towards his travel costs, and the other constituent members helped to cover the other costs of the Secretariat. Another step forward had been taken.

Neither Archbishop Clarizio nor Monsignor Frayne of the Pontifical Commission for the Pastoral Care of Migrants and Itinerant People was able to be present at this conference, which was a source of much regret. Archbishop Clarizio sent a very full greeting, and the conference recorded its 'deep appreciation of the unique contribution made by Monsignor Frayne towards the foundation of the I.C.M.A. and to its development over the first year.'

The theme of the conference, which was attended by 107 participants and made most welcome by Danish Church and State authorities, was 'The Personal and Family Implications of Being a Seafarer'. Among many memorable features was a very moving paper delivered by a Roman Catholic deacon, Bernard Vincent, who was sailing as an engine room mechanic on ships with 'Third World' crews. He graphically highlighted some of the problems experienced by seafarers from developing countries, particularly on 'flag of convenience' ships. The atmosphere of the conference, to which the beauty of its setting contributed much, was uplifting, and the strength of the desire for increased working together was apparent in a unanimously agreed minute which recorded that 'the I.C.M.A. must become a reality at port and regional level, and that member organisations with staff in ports where other member organisations work should meet regularly to plan co-operation and avoid duplication of effort. Such local co-operation would make the I.C.M.A. meaningful.'[8]

Making I.C.M.A. meaningful was the task to which Tom Kerfoot devoted himself in the next six years. It was a busy time. In his report to the 1978 plenary conference, held in New York under the chairmanship of a Dutch pastor, Jacob Leij, he was able to record increasing worldwide observance of Sea Sunday (the day when Churches of all denominations all over the world are invited to focus their thoughts, prayers and worship on seafarers and the maritime scene); the establishment, through the good offices of the International Transport Workers Federation, of an International Council for Seamen's Welfare, in which I.C.M.A. would play a full part along with the International Transport Workers Federation, the International Shipping Federation, the International Labour Organisation and governmental and municipal welfare agencies; and the preparation of a second edition of the Directory of seafarers' centres and agencies. He had represented I.C.M.A. as an official observer at the 62nd Maritime Session of the International Labour Conference and at the 16th World Congress of the Apostleship of the Sea in Hong Kong. At port, national and regional level there was increasing collaboration, and he referred to a number of informal groupings at regional and port level which, while not operating under the aegis of the I.C.M.A., nevertheless owed their origins to the new spirit which had been born and the personal associations which had developed between members of the Association. A regular bulletin, 'I.C.M.A. News', was being circulated. He identified a number of important maritime issues to which members should devote attention, and advised the conference that the Standing Committee was planning to meet for two days without a business agenda in order to review the working of

I.C.M.A. not only to make it 'more lively and effective' but also to 'build on the foundations already laid and continue in the spirit that gave the movement birth'. He reported that he was working three full days a week, but those who knew him well were aware that he was giving I.C.M.A. his undivided attention. He stressed the fact that I.C.M.A. was by deliberate intention a free association of its members, and not a kind of super directing agency; his role was to be 'the servant of the servants of the Lord'.

The New York conference, which was attended by 154 delegates from 17 maritime countries, considered the theme 'Christ in the Maritime World—evangelism and pastoral care of seafarers'. It was memorable for some excellent papers, of which that by Oddvar Michaelsen (the Foreign Secretary of the Norwegian Seamen's Mission) stood out, a plenary session in which Bishop Rene Gracida, Episcopal Promotor of the Apostleship of the Sea in the United States of America, and Bishop Bruce Evans, Liaison Bishop of The Missions to Seamen in the Church of the Province of South Africa, spoke of their work, and some typically warm North American hospitality. It said goodbye to The Revd. Johannes Aardal, the representative of the Council of the Nordic Seamen's Missions, who was retiring. Johannes was a key figure in the foundation of I.C.M.A., and the conference 'recorded its deep appreciation of (his) great personal contribution' and the thanks of I.C.M.A. 'to one who had shared so much from the wealth of his experience as a pastor and leader in the Nordic Missions'.

Between the plenary conferences of New York in 1978 and Berlin in 1981, and under the chairmanship of The Revd. Carl Osterwald (General Secretary of the German Seamen's Mission), I.C.M.A. continued to make steady progress. The resolutions of the New York conference were energetically followed up and implemented as fully as possible, though problems were encountered with one, namely the setting up of a multi-language, ecumenically based fellowship of Christian seafarers. The biennial inter-confessional South East Asia conference of seafarers' chaplains expressed a desire to become a regional organisation of I.C.M.A. A third edition of the Directory of seafarers' centres and agencies was published in 1980. Members of the Standing Committee undertook visits to ports and places where new needs for ministry to seafarers had been identified and reported back to the Committee. A picture of cohesive maritime ministry was emerging.

The plenary conference held in Berlin in 1981, and attended by 147 delegates from 18 countries, was marked by a splendid atmosphere, good fellowship, and a never-to-be-forgotten visit to East Berlin. The conference theme was 'Pastoral Issues in the life of the seafarer today', and major introductory papers were delivered on 'Seafarers and their families—wishes and anxieties' and 'Alcohol—joy and danger to mankind'. The Revd. Dr. Paul Chapman spoke about his work with the newly created Center for Seafarers' Rights in New York, and high-lighted an issue which was causing concern to seafarers' chaplains all over the world. The visit to East Berlin, where a number of pastors and lay people from many parts of the German Democratic Republic had assembled to meet the delegates, was notable for an inspiring address by Professor Dietrich Affeld, Lay President of the Lutheran Assembly of the German Democratic Republic. He spoke of what it meant to be a committed Christian in a Communist country.[9]

The conference resolutions included, inter alia, a call to members to make every effort to ensure that their governments ratified the International Labour Organisation's Convention 147, which calls on the country of registry of a ship to set and enforce standards of ship safety and crew competency, and upon the port of call country to take measures necessary to rectify conditions hazardous to safety and health. They also gave encouragement and support to the special human rights project of the Seamen's Church Institute of New York and New Jersey, urging members to develop an informal network to share information and to support one another in this field.

The conference also received formal notice of Tom Ker-foot's intention to retire as General Secretary in 1982. His close friend of many years, Monsignor Denis McGuinness, paid tribute to this remarkable man whose vision, energy, enthusiasm and eirenic nature meant so much to I.C.M.A., and the conference rose to its feet to express its appreciation of a respected, trusted and much-loved friend.

The retirement of Tom Kerfoot led I.C.M.A. to take another large step of faith. It was clear that the task of making I.C.M.A. meaningful at every level of the maritime world was gradually being achieved, that the work of the secretariat was steadily increasing, and that the next General Secretary should be appointed on a full-time basis and have a self-contained office. It was equally clear that such an appointment would involve the member organisations in considerable extra expense, and that they would have to commit themselves to providing it if they felt it right to go ahead. The decision to appoint a full-time General Secretary was taken unanimously.

After thorough consultation The Revd. Bernard Krug was appointed. A German Lutheran who had spent the first four years after the Second World War in the Soviet Union as a prisoner of war, Bernard was senior chaplain of the inter-confessional Felixstowe International Seafarers' Centre at the time of his appointment. He had welded together a happy and effective team of chaplains of different denominations, back-grounds and ages, and the centre was flourishing. He was in his mid 50's, physically very fit, and blessed with abundant energy. His parent organisation, the German Seamen's Mission, gave strong support to his appointment by offering to continue to pay his salary and allowing him to continue to live in and work from his chaplaincy house. This most generous offer was warmly welcomed and gratefully accepted.

He took up his new responsibilities in the middle of 1982 at the same time as the writer became Chairman of the Standing Committee, and at once set about familiarising himself with worldwide maritime ministry. He travelled extensively to meet people, assess situations, and see at first hand what the Churches were doing and how they were doing it. He initiated a wide correspondence and the computerisation of the infor-mation contained in the Directory of seafarers' centres and agencies. He thoroughly perused Tom Kerfoot's admirably comprehensive files. He won the respect and affection of seafarers' chaplains and people involved in ministering to seafarers everywhere by his friendliness, his capacity for hard work, his willingness to speak and be spoken to plainly, and his sheer joy in his task.

The years immediately before the fifth plenary conference held in the Philippines in 1985 were a period of growth and expansion of I.C.M.A.'s work, based on the solid foundations laid in previous years. Regional groups were established in the Mediterranean, the United Kingdom and Northern Europe, and each region held its first inter-confessional conference in

1984. Bernard Krug was invited to address the Council of Nordic Seamen's Missions, and spoke about international and inter-confessional co-operation. He attended the annual conferences of the International Council of Seamen's Agencies, itself the North American and Caribbean outreach of I.C.M.A. He made two important and successful visits to the Philippines to prepare the way for the 1985 plenary conference, and the very fact that the conference was held there at a difficult time in the country's history was a great tribute to his work. The country was moving inexorably towards the overthrow of President Marcos, the Roman Catholic Church was speaking openly of 'the Parliament of the Streets', and there was little active ministry to seafarers. The decision to hold the conference there was made because the Standing Committee recognised its responsibility to afford members an opportunity to experience at first hand the life and background of the country supplying the largest number of seafarers serving on 'flag of convenience' ships, and because the Roman Catholic Church was so warmly welcoming and gave such positive assistance.

The theme of the 1985 plenary conference was 'Changes in the seafaring world', and focused the attention of the 154 delegates on Asia, the home of more than two thirds of today's seafarers. It was a remarkable conference. It gave many of the participants their first experience of life in a developing country. Many of the speakers were Asian. Accommodation for many of the delegates was basic. There was an excellent atmosphere. The vitality and influence of the Roman Catholic Church was apparent everywhere. The Honorary President of the Conference was the leader of the Roman Catholic Church in the Philippines, Cardinal Jaime Sin, who took a keen interest in its daily deliberations, and invited all the delegates to meals in 'The House of Sin'[10] at the beginning and the end. Bishop Gabriel Reyes, chairman of the (Roman Catholic) Episcopal Commission on Migration and Tourism in Manila, was Co-Chairman of the conference: he was a wise counsellor, a friend to all, and the link with the Cardinal.

A constantly recurring theme in the deliberations was the unjust treatment experienced by many Filipino seafarers serving on 'flag of convenience' ships. Seafarers' chaplains throughout the world had personal knowledge of this, and when officials from the Philippine Overseas Employment

Administration (the government agency controlling Filipino contract workers, including seafarers, serving overseas) came to address the conference and answer questions, a very lively session ensued. The conference adopted two comprehensive and specific resolutions referring to unsatisfactory conditions of employment for Filipino seafarers, and Cardinal Sin personally conveyed these to the authorities at the highest level. Among other resolutions was one re-affirming I.C.M.A.'s 'support and recognition of the achievement of the Center for Seafarers' Rights and urging all member organisations to distribute its information booklets.' The media coverage of the end of conference press briefing showed beyond all doubt that I.C.M.A. had become a very meaningful organisation.

In the years since that plenary conference Bernard Krug and other representatives of I.C.M.A. and of the Center for Seafarers' Rights have returned to the Philippines on several occasions for follow-up meetings with the Philippine Overseas Employment Administration, the manning agencies who recruit Filipino seafarers to serve on overseas registered ships, and other interested organisations. In December 1987 I.C.M.A. sponsored a Maritime Manning Conference in Manila. It was attended by government officials, a number of manning agents, and representatives of seafarers' organisations in the Philippines, and it produced a 'Code of Good Practice for Manning Agents', a model document of its kind.

In 1987 member organisations carried out a 'Seafarers' Survey' in order to obtain a comprehensive overall picture of seafaring today. Chaplaincy staff in 59 ports all over the world put 30 questions to 4525 seafarers from 98 different nations. 43% of the surveys were completed on board ship and 57% ashore. The questions had been translated into a number of languages. The survey was confidential: seafarers were not asked to give their names or the names of their ships or employers. The questions covered family matters, reasons for taking up seafaring as a career, fair treatment at sea, payment of commissions to obtain a job at sea, length of contract, registration of ship, religious affiliations, church attendance, and use of seafarers' centres. The survey was a great success: the questions were willingly and fully answered by a wide cross-section of seafarers in an exercise never previously attempted on so wide a scale in the seafaring world. The

information the survey produced will be of enormous assistance in planning the future. It was pleasing in that it revealed
that a very high proportion of seafarers make use of Christian
seafarers' centres, and that a substantial majority of those
questioned considered that they had been fairly treated during
their seagoing careers. It also revealed areas where Christian
organisations must concentrate their efforts, and notably on
the significant number of seafarers who experience unjust
treatment.

Plenary and regional conferences of I.C.M.A. have regularly
aroused a healthy frustration with the ecclesiastical disciplines
which prevent Christians of all denominations from sharing
together in the sacrament of Holy Communion. It is hard to be
asked not to receive the elements because it may cause embar-
rassment to someone in authority. It is hard not to be able to
share in the deepest act of Christian fellowship with people
with whom daily worship, prayer, planning and work is
shared. Ordained and lay people alike experience great distress
that at the altar, where we should be most united, we are most
divided. At times the rules are quite simply laid aside, and the
resulting fellowship at the deepest level gives an inspiring but
tantalising glimpse of the glory of the unity which Our Lord
Jesus Christ wills for His Church.

At the North American Maritime Ministries Conference
held in Corpus Christi, Texas, in 1985, the 120 or so delegates
representing most of the major Christian denominations
attended a daily joint celebration of the Mass and Holy
Communion. 'There were two altars, one for Roman Catholics and one for everybody else. We started the service
separately, then all came together for the Ministry of the
Word—the reading of the Epistle, the saying of a responsorial
psalm, the reading of the Gospel, a short address and the
intercessions. Then we returned to our separate altars for the
confession, absolution and prayer of consecration. We broke
the bread simultaneously and said the words of the Greeting of
Peace. Then we all then greeted each other . . . before returning
to receive the sacrament at our own altar. Finally, we finished
the service together with the blessing and a hymn. After some
teething troubles on the first day the joint celebration was
wonderful. It was dignified, happy, moving—and deeply painful. Our unhappy divisions were starkly presented. Yet we

were, and are, on the road towards that unity which Our Lord Jesus Christ wants for His Church.'[12] What had already been achieved was plain for all to see: so was what remains to be achieved.

Two questions can now be asked. What has I.C.M.A. accomplished? What is the way ahead for I.C.M.A.?

I.C.M.A.'s actual and potential contribution to the life of the Church as a whole should be assessed in the light of what it has already accomplished. It has provided meeting points for people of all backgrounds engaged in maritime ministry at all levels in many parts of the world. It has provided opportunities for Christians to exchange ideas and experience, share spiritual insights, learn more of different Christian traditions, worship together, discuss matters of common importance, and formulate jointly agreed policies. It has promoted understanding between denominations, and inter-confessional and international collaboration. It has paved the way for inter-confessional and international collaboration at grass roots level in ports in many parts of the world. It speaks as the collective and respected voice of its member organisations, yet remains their servant. Its strength lies in the fact that it remains a free association of Christian organisations.

I.C.M.A. now has long, varied and extensive experience of inter-confessional and international collaboration. Seafarers' chaplains are daily involved in witnessing to, and engaging in, dialogue with people of widely different faiths and cultures. They exercise pastoral, prophetic and evangelistic roles in the shipping world. The partnership between ordained and lay Christians in maritime ministry is one of its great strengths. It is this living and growing experience in all these aspects of ministry that I.C.M.A. has to offer to the Church as a whole and to the individual Churches.

The way ahead for I.C.M.A. must surely be to continue to build on the solid foundations which were laid in Rotterdam in 1969. At the plenary conference of I.C.M.A. held in the Philippines in 1985 the writer said this:

'1. I.C.M.A. must go on furthering the cause of interconfessional collaboration and the promotion of unity among Christians. Ours will be a unity in diversity, not uniformity, and we must go on working for it and towards it.

2. I.C.M.A. must always build on its spiritual foundation. Our fellowship in Christ must be reflected in a growing and deepening life together. We must share with each other the riches of our different traditions.

3. I.C.M.A. must get across to the individual Churches and the Church as a whole the message of what has been achieved in inter-confessional collaboration in the field of seafarers' ministry. There is much to be done . . .

4. I.C.M.A. must keep pace with change. It must grapple with the major issues of the day, like seafarers' rights and Christian unity.

5. It must expand its vision of ministry to include everybody involved in shipping at every level.

6. It must go on establishing regional branches, and

7. It must do its best to involve as fully as possible all who belong to the organisations of which it is comprised. We need to become more member-participative.'

Since 1986 the Chairman of the Standing Committee has been The Revd. Dr. Jim Whittemore, Director of the Seamen's Church Institute of New York and New Jersey. Under his wise and strong leadership the International Christian Maritime Association has gone from strength to strength.

Notes

1. Quoted by Roald Kverndal in an address entitled 'Where Have We Come From?' and delivered to the North American Maritime Ministries Conference held at Corpus Christ, Texas, in October 1985. Dr. Kverdal is the Executive Secretary of the International Council of Seamen's Agencies in North America.

2. I am greatly indebted to Pastor Jacob Schokking for a copy of a translation of his address at the opening service of the International Consultation on Services to Seafarers and also for a very full and fascinating letter setting out his impressions of the Consultation.

3. J. Schokking, letter of 24.1.1988 addressed to the writer.

4. Ibid.

5. Ibid.

6. I am similarly indebted to Pastor Johannes Aardal for much help and his written reflections on the Consultation. The passage quoted here is taken from a letter addressed to the writer on 11.11.1987.

7. I.C.M.A. Report on First Plenary Conference, London, 31st July–4th August 1972, page 3.

8. I.C.M.A. Report on Second Plenary Conference, Denmark, 7th–11th July 1975, page 11.

9. The full text of Professor Affeld's remarkably courageous address is printed in the I.C.M.A. 'Fourth Plenary Conference, Berlin' report. The conference was held between July 12th and 18th, 1981.

10. This was the Cardinal's own reference to his home, made in his introductory and closing remarks addressed to delegates, and quoted in the I.C.M.A.'s 'Plenary Conference 1985, The Philippines' Report on pages 1 and 66.

11. The Code is set out in full on pages 16 and 17 of I.C.M.A.'s 'Maritime Manning Conference, Manila 7–9 December 1987, report.

12. Extract from my Report as the General Secretary of the Missions to Seamen, September/October 1985.

VIII The Extent and Variety of Maritime Ministry Today

'There are varieties of gifts, but the same Spirit. There are varieties of service, but the same Lord. There are many forms of work, but all of them, in all men, are the work of the same God.'

St. Paul's 1st Letter to the Corinthians, Chapter 12, verses 4 to 6.

Between them the Christian Churches provide ministry to seafarers in 940 ports all over the world. The nature of the ministry varies from port to port, organisation to organisation and individual to individual. For the past twenty-five years it has been the writer's joy and privilege as a seafarers' chaplain, and more recently as a pastor of seafarers' chaplains, to see much of this work at first hand and to be closely involved in some of it. When the whole range of this ministry is studied and assessed an extraordinarily rich and impressive picture emerges.

There are many factors which influence the establishment and development of maritime ministry in a particular port. The size, layout and location of the harbour in relation to the nearest centre of population determines whether or not a seafarers' centre is required, and if so where it should be sited. The number of ships using the port, the length of time they spend there, and the numbers of seafarers on board, determine the size of the seafarers' centre. Climatic conditions influence the design. The vitality of the local congregations, the strength of their desire to work together, the extent to which local goodwill can be harnessed to the project, and the amount of money which can be raised, are all important elements in the establishment of ministry to seafarers.

On a world scene in which there are 940 ports where there is Christian ministry to seafarers, some 1300 individual chaplaincies, and 100 residential and 250 non-residential seafarers'

centres,[1] it is obviously unrealistic to attempt to describe each
and every chaplaincy, ministry and seafarers' centre. What is
possible, however, is to present a selection of widely different
ministries undertaken by various organisations in different
parts of the world, and in so doing portray a glimpse of the
total picture. It is making the selection of which among so
many marvellous ministries to write about that presents the
greatest difficulty!*

Fos
A Roman Catholic initiative in a remote port

The port of Marseilles-Fos in the South of France ranks as the
sixth largest port in the world in terms of tonnage of cargo
handled. It spreads over a distance of some fifty miles: there are
135 long-established berths in Marseilles itself, three vast new
man-made harbour complexes between thirty and fifty miles
to the West near the small town of Fos, and some oil terminals
between Marseilles and Fos.

The development of the port of Fos began in the late 1960's.
Its three complexes were designed to handle containerised
cargo, bulk cargo, oil, chemicals, natural gas and dry cargo,
including motor vehicles and steel. They were built in an area
where there are no large centres of population, no passenger
rail services and no regular bus services to the new harbours.
For seafarers whose ships berthed at the new terminals the
difficulties of getting ashore for a break were daunting—
the ships were loaded or discharged very swiftly, the nearest
town or village was some distance away, taxi fares were
astronomical, and there were no chaplains visiting the ships
to offer a welcome, information, counsel or transport.

Late in 1974 the writer sailed from Fremantle in Western
Australia to Tilbury in England on the 28,000 ton container
ship 'Discovery Bay', which made a twelve hour stop in Fos to
discharge several hundred containers. The ship berthed three
miles from the small town of Port St. Louis du Rhône. The only
visitors were people with official business. It was a cold, wet
and miserable day. After more than three weeks at sea a
number of people on board decided to take a trip ashore.

* These situations are described as they were in the middle of 1988; it is recognised
that they change constantly.

Experiencing the frustrations of an absence of public transport, being viewed with indifference as a stranger in a strange
land, having to buy a drink in order to get out of the rain and
into the warm, and feeling a general lack of welcome, caused
the writer to think how differently the people of Malta greeted
Saint Paul and his companions after their shipwreck, and how
in hundreds of ports around the world today the Churches
provide a warm welcome to seafarers. The need for a ministry
to seafarers in Fos was apparent.

But while the need was apparent, the way to meet it was not.

In 1981 the Archbishop of Marseilles, Cardinal Roger
Etchegaray, published a paper expressing his concern at the
lack of ministry to seafarers throughout the port, and in 1984
the International Christian Maritime Association, at its first
Mediterranean regional consultation, 'welcomed the concern
of the Cardinal Archbishop of Marseilles for the provision of
an ecumenical ministry to seafarers in Fos and Marseilles', and
suggested that a feasibility study to determine what sort of
ministry might be appropriate should be made.

In 1986 the Roman Catholic organisation La Mission de la
Mer, and another called Les Amis des Marins, rented a house
at Port de Bouc near Fos with the intention of adapting it for
use as a seafarers' centre serving the 4000 ships a year now
calling at Fos. The dioceses of Marseilles and Aix-en-Provence
accepted responsibility for the salary of the leader of the
project, Father Philippe Plantevin, a member of La Mission de
France, which is an order of worker priests. With willing
voluntary assistance from other worker priests and lay people
work began on the conversion of the house. The (Anglican)
Missions to Seamen, with whom Les Amis des Marins work in
happy partnership in Dunkerque, joyfully accepted an invitation to be a partner in the ministry. Substantial grants for the
purchase of the necessary building materials, furniture and a
minibus were generously made available by the International
Transport Workers Federation, and on November 27th 1986
the centre was officially opened.

It has proved to be a godsend. The provision of the minibus
means that seafarers can now come to the centre without the
expense of a taxi fare, which from most remote berths costs as
much for the return journey as a rail ticket from Marseilles to
Paris, more than 500 miles away! At the centre seafarers can

cook themselves a meal in the kitchen, there are two telephone boxes, a shop/bar/canteen/foreign exchange counter, a comfortable lounge, a library/paperback book area and an emergency/guest bedroom. There is also accommodation for the chaplain and a student assistant. All the helpers are volunteers, many of whom are accompanied by members of their family, the centre is being well used, and a ministry to seafarers in a very remote port is being provided.

Port Walcott
A remote port—a Local and Anglican initiative

Port Walcott is situated on the North coast of Western Australia, 21° South of the Equator, 1000 miles North of Perth, and between the busy ports of Dampier and Port Hedland. It is the port through which the Cliffs Robe River Iron Ore Associates company exports the iron ore it mines in the hinterland.

It is a hot, sticky, remote port, over which a thick cloud of pervasive brown iron ore dust usually hangs.

The port came into being in 1972, and consists of a jetty protruding 1.6 miles out to sea. The large bulk carriers of more than 200,000 deadweight tons which call there berth on either side of the seaward end of the jetty, and only two ships can be handled at any one time. Their length of stay is up to three days and depends on whether there is only one ship being worked at the time. Around 120 ships, taking out more than 15 million tons of iron ore, call annually.

From the time the port opened there were serious problems facing seafarers wanting to go ashore. Because of the extreme heat, the moving conveyor belts, and the height of the jetty above the water, the company wisely forbade seafarers to walk along the jetty and insisted that they should travel in authorised vehicles. At the landward end of the jetty, the road to the main gate is two and a half miles long and passes through the iron ore terminal, which consists of a crushing plant, rail truck-tipping machinery, conveyor belts and a stockpile of ore. From the main gate to the small company town of Wickham the distance is a further five miles.

A number of people working in the port, some officials of

Cliffs Robe River Iron Ore Associates, and many local residents, were concerned about the isolation of the seafarers in the port, and they set up a committee, the Port Walcott Seafarers' Project, to see what they could do to improve conditions for them. They were joined by The Revd. Ted Cosens, who had arrived as port chaplain of The Missions to Seamen in Dampier in 1976 and whose brief included assisting in any way he could at Port Walcott, and received much sound advice and assistance from The Revd. Terry Ranson, Senior Chaplain of The Missions to Seamen in Fremantle and State Secretary of The Missions to Seamen for Western Australia. The committee suggested that seafarers might be allowed to use the facilities of the Wickham Social Club, and that an extension might be added to the Club to provide special amenities for seafarers. They would obtain transport to convey seafarers between their ships and the Club and recruit volunteer drivers.

Their plans were welcomed by the company, the port staff, the Social Club, the Churches and the seafarers themselves. All the money for the project was raised locally, the building work was carried out by volunteers, the purchase of a bus was generously subsidised by the company, and a team of volunteer drivers was organised. On October 21st 1982 the writer was greatly honoured by being invited to open the Port Walcott Seafarers' Centre.

The Centre consists of an L-shaped room which has telephone facilities, a shop counter and a comfortable lounge. It is staffed by volunteers who open it whenever ships are in port. In the first ten months after it opened more than 1000 seafarers were brought to the centre by the volunteer drivers. The swimming pool, bar, restaurant and other facilities of the adjoining Social Club were all made available to seafarers, who could thus be made welcome by the local community. The Anglican parish priest of Roebourne willingly acts as Honorary Chaplain of The Missions to Seamen, under whose auspices the centre operates.

The whole operation is simple and straightforward. It owes much to the vision, enthusiasm, common sense and hard work of the Harbour Master, Captain Bob Hudson, and his helpers, who were ably led by 'Snowy' Goldstraw; and the Church was always there in support.

Napier/Hawke's Bay
A local ecumenical initiative

The port of Napier is situated on the East coast of the North Island of New Zealand in Hawke's Bay, 39° South of the Equator. It is a busy, compact, well-equipped small port, with eight major berths capable of handling ships drawing up to 36 feet (11 metres) of water.

In the second half of the 1970's an Anglican industrial chaplain in Napier, The Revd. Dr. Rod Falconer, became concerned that in a port handling some 250 ships and more than a million tons of cargo a year there was no regular ministry to seafarers. He shared his concerns with the Dean of the Cathedral in Napier, The Very Revd. Brian Davis (now Archbishop of New Zealand), and in 1977 the writer made a visit to Napier and discussed with them both what kind of ministry and facilities would be appropriate and how finance might be raised.

By 1980, when the writer paid a second visit, a great deal of preparatory work had been done. An excellent relationship between Dr. Rod Falconer and the Hawke's Bay Harbour Board had been established, a suitable plot of land for a seafarers' centre had been allocated by the Harbour Board and New Zealand Railways, a steering committee for the projected seafarers' centre, including an Anglican representative, a Roman Catholic representative and the secretary of the local Council of Churches, had been set up, and the local Church authorities and the seafarers' societies had been kept fully informed about the project and had signified their approval of it. Detailed plans for the seafarers' centre had been drawn up, and a firm tender for building it had been obtained. The Central Office of The Missions to Seamen in London was requested to initiate and support an application to the International Transport Workers Federation for financial assistance. When the International Transport Workers Federation, through the good offices of its representatives in New Zealand, indicated that it would contribute half the total cost of building and equipping the centre, the project seemed to be progressing very satisfactorily.

Then, as so often happens with any new enterprise, a number of serious obstacles appeared. The site originally allocated for the centre could not in fact be made available, and another—far better in the event!—had to be negotiated. Then The Revd. Dr. Rod Falconer, a key person, moved to an appointment in Auckland, and the prospect of raising half the capital cost of the centre, as well as running it when it was completed, assumed a daunting appearance for the good people on the steering committee, who had had no previous experience of such work.

It was at this point, in 1982, that the Apostleship of the Sea, the British Sailors' Society and The Missions to Seamen came to the rescue. Together they guaranteed the other half of the capital cost of the centre, and suddenly the way ahead was clear and exciting. During a visit to Napier in that year the writer discussed with the members of the steering committee and the new Honorary Chaplain of The Missions to Seamen, The Revd. Noel Hendery, the provision of training for the Honorary Chaplains who would serve the centre, the appointment of a competent person to handle the day-to-day financial and administrative operation of the centre, and the provision of training for the voluntary helpers. The willingness to assist of The Revd. Ted Cosens, National Chaplain of The Missions to Seamen, Father Barney Bourke, National Director of the Apostleship of the Sea, and Mrs. Shirley Farquahar, Secretary of the British Sailors' Society in New Zealand, was a great bonus.

On September 10th 1983 the new Hawke's Bay Seafarers' Centre was officially opened, and 'behind that simple statement lies a story of the vision of a number of people, of a combination of hope, optimism, frustration, disappointment and ultimately delight in achievement, and of a great deal of determination and hard work'.[2] Ideally situated close to the entrance to the port on the road into town, which is no more than 7 or 8 minutes walk away, the centre is a most attractive building and commands a magnificent view of the Pacific Ocean less than 100 yards away.

Right from the outset the centre has been well used. In the first year of operation almost 5000 seafarers made use of its facilities, and more than 1000 international telephone calls were put through for seafarers. It soon became clear that extensions were needed to the small well-designed premises, and the necessary finance was generated by the centre's activities.

After a visit in 1984 the writer reported that 'a feature of the work of the Centre is that NOBODY is salaried—there is no wage bill at all. There are 9 Honorary Chaplains (7 ordained and 2 lay), a committee of management and a good band of dedicated voluntary workers. It might be thought that without at least one full-time staff member co-ordinating the whole operation confusion and chaos might reign supreme, but such is not the case: the whole operation is run on admirably orderly lines . . . The total absence of paid staff is an almost revoluntionary concept in a centre of this size and activity, but it shows what can be done. Congratulations to all the Churches in Napier for achieving so much.'[3]

Hong Kong
A Large and Comprehensive Operation
An Anglican Initiative—an Inter-confessional Partnership

Hong Kong is one of the great ports of the world. Situated on the South coast of mainland China, 22° North of the Equator, it has long been a highly important centre of international trade, commerce and finance. It is one of the world's main gateways to China.

The Missions to Seamen has been at work in Hong Kong since 1885 and has been served by a succession of fine chaplains and lay staff. Its affairs have been wisely and imaginatively guided by dedicated committee members from a wide variety of professional backgrounds.

In the early 1960's the Society sold its premises on Hong Kong Island and built the present Mariners' Club in Kowloon on the mainland. It was, and is, a magnificent seafarers' centre. A tall building situated in a prime position in the heart of the business, commercial and tourist life of Kowloon, it has five floors of residential accommodation of various types for seafarers of different backgrounds, cultures and lifestyles. It also has a fine swimming pool, a ten pin bowling alley, a superb restaurant, an excellent functions room, a shop, haircut saloon, snack bar and bars. The chapel, dedicated to St. Peter, is the hub of the Club's life, for here day by day Anglican, Roman Catholic and Lutheran chaplains come together to commit themselves and their work to the Living Lord.

In 1969 the Roman Catholic Apostleship of the Sea accepted an invitation from The Missions to Seamen and the Committee of Management of the Mariners' Club to work together in partnership from the Mariners' Club. The agreement had the wholehearted approval of the hierarchies of both Churches and heralded a new era of inter-confessional collaboration. In January 1970 'Anglican Holy Communion and Catholic Mass were celebrated together on the last day of the Octave of prayer for Christian unity. There was a congregation of between 75 and 80, and 23 Anglican seamen communicated and 7 Roman Catholic seamen. Two altars were designed and constructed and set on either side of the main altar in the chapel. The main altar was used as a credence table, and Father Georges and I both took wine and wafers from the same cruets and ciborium . . . The service was beautiful, very moving, but perhaps too powerful. My sermon drew attention to the defect in this ecumenical occasion, and for many people the division was extremely painful. Many cried after the service. Father Fedele said that during the service he couldn't talk, he couldn't sing. The sight of the two altars was too painful, and most of the time he could see only the one white altar shining in the centre; afterwards he said that he thought that this was a vision of the future . . . Neither of our Bishops gave authority for this occasion, and neither could they. These were two separate celebrations held in the same church at the same time.'[4] The partnership between Anglicans and Roman Catholics went from strength to strength—as did the feeling of utter frustration that at the altar they could still not be totally together.

In 1981 the Danish Seamen's Church accepted an invitation to join the partnership in ministry, and their first pastor, The Revd. Ronald Pedersen, made an immediate and important contribution to the life and work of the chaplaincy team. His successors have been equally valuable members of the whole set-up.

In the early 1970's a new container terminal was established at Kwai Chung, some ten miles from Kowloon in the New Territories. With admirable wisdom and foresight the Committee of the Mariners' Club, under the chairmanship of Mr. David Newbigging (then of Jardine Matheson and now Chairman of the General Committee of The Missions to Seamen in

London), augmented by representation of the Apostleship of the Sea, decided to press ahead with planning and building a second seafarers' centre to serve this new and important facility. Opened in 1975, the Mariners' Club in Kwai Chung soon began to meet a great need. Much smaller than the centre in Kowloon, it provides recreational facilities, a restaurant, bar, chapel and medical and dental practices—an imaginative and much appreciated service at a terminal where ships spend very little time and which was a frustrating journey away from Kowloon when the centre was built.

The pastoral ministry of ship visiting in the port of Hong Kong is carried out by launch, except at the container terminal. Most of the ships load or discharge cargo into smaller craft, and the only way to visit them is by launch. The Missions to Seamen has had a succession of launches, the last being 'Dayspring V', a two deck vessel with a crew of four and capable of carrying 30 people, and the Apostleship of the Sea brought to the partnership a small boat called 'Stella Maris', the only vessel (in the writer's knowledge) to fly the Vatican flag. In 1987 a new launch, which for bureaucratic reasons had to be named 'Mariners' Club', replaced both; faster, slightly smaller than 'Dayspring V', she is a symbol of the way the shipping industry is moving on.

The current chaplaincy team is very ably led by The Revd. Wally Andrews, a gifted priest with 26 years experience of ministry to seafarers in a number of ports. The two Roman Catholic priests who contributed so much to the establishment of the partnership are no longer there—Father Georges Dopchie died suddenly in 1987, and Father Dan Fitzpatrick has retired to Australia. In their very different ways both made a great contribution to the world of maritime ministry.

The work of the chaplaincy team is supplemented and complemented by the Family Service Unit, which was introduced in 1976 with the aim of providing a practical and advisory service to Chinese seafarers and their families. It is run by two highly qualified Chinese Christian women social workers who work in association with, and under the direction of, the chaplains. They produce a regular newsletter for Chinese seafarers and their families, and organise group activities, such as swimming classes, summer launch parties and a children's 'fun day'. They offer expert counsel, advice and

assistance to seafarers in hospital or with personal or contractual problems, and have made a great impact on the Hong
Kong shipping scene.

The committee of management of the Mariners' Clubs have
been very concerned to keep both centres fully up-to-date, and
the recent comprehensive refurbishment of both has made
them as good as any seafarers' centres in the world. The quality
and range of services they offer is a tribute to the efforts of the
committee, the chaplains, and the management team led by
Mr. Alastair Hall and Mr. Wong Kam Moon.

Both centres are very well used.

Santos
Home Missions Operating in Difficult Conditions

The port of Santos, 24° South of the Equator on the East coast
of Brazil, is situated 40 miles South of Sao Paulo, the country's
largest centre of population and one of the biggest cities in the
world.

It is a busy port, reputedly the busiest in South America in
terms of the numbers of ships handled, but this is not easy to
confirm because of the reluctance of the authorities in some
South American countries to release statistics. Its 65 berths,
some of them capable of handling ships of up to 70,000
deadweight tons, stretch over a distance of 10 miles. As an
indication of its trade the statistics for the first six months of
1986 are illuminating. During that period 2016 ships visited
the port, of which 1315 were general cargo vessels, 332 were
tankers, 265 were bulk carriers, 22 were passenger ships, and
the remainder of miscellaneous types. 75% were registered
outside Brazil. Cargoes imported included raw materials, oil,
chemicals, liquid gases, fertilisers and grain, while exports
included coffee, motor vehicles, sugar, grain, soya beans and
flour, fruit and concentrated orange juice.

The provision of ministry to seafarers serving on merchant
ships calling at the port has been difficult at times in recent
years. The writer made visits to Brazil in 1975, 1977, 1981,
1984 and 1986, and has observed the various maritime
chaplaincies in Santos at first hand.

The major cause of the difficulties experienced by seafarers' chaplains, both Brazilian and expatriate, has been the reluctance of the authorities to grant passes for the chaplains to visit ships in port, and their unwillingness to allow chaplains who are permitted to visit ships to drive a motor vehicle into the docks. No doubt they have good reasons for their caution, and the writer would wish to record at once his appreciation of a comprehensive tour of the port on board a tug in 1977; it enabled him to obtain a clear picture of the layout and nature of the port.

The effect of these restrictions has been that the four Christian organisations serving seafarers in Santos have not been able to carry out their work as freely as they would have wished. The Apostleship of the Sea has splendid premises which are only now realising their potential after a number of years during which their clergy were unable to obtain dock passes. The Norwegian Seamen's Mission has a beautiful centre which serves both seafarers and expatriates resident in Brazil; its chaplain is a member of the Norwegian diplomatic corps, and so has no problem in obtaining permission to visit ships. The German Seamen's Mission, which since the mid 1970's has worked in close association with a German-speaking Lutheran congregation in Santos, has had some problems over obtaining permission to visit ships, and The Missions to Seamen, which has been at work in Santos since 1915 and is closely linked with All Saints Church there, has also had difficulties.

The same four organisations have also found that their lack of complete freedom of operation has slowed down the process of growing together which has been a feature of maritime ministry in other parts of the world during the last twenty years. The chaplains seldom meet in the course of ship visiting, they are physically unable to visit every ship they are permitted to go to because of the necessity to proceed only on foot within the docks, and they cannot realistically contemplate working together from one or maybe two centres unless and until they can feel a greater sense of security and permanence in their ministry.

In these frustrating circumstances each of the four centres does excellent work in its own way. The Norwegian and German Seamen's Missions both serve seafarers and expatriates living locally in really lovely, attractive premises. The

Apostleship of the Sea carries out a most effective ministry among the fishing community, and to a lesser extent in the merchant shipping scene. Only now is their excellent centre beginning to fulfil its potential. The Missions to Seamen has a beautiful 'Home Mission' where the chaplain, The Revd. Frank Snedker, and his wife Betty welcome 600 seafarers every month. Frank and Betty have been in Santos since the present 'Flying Angel House' was purchased in 1968, and have become a living legend to thousands of seafarers of many nationalities who have visited the port and the house. 'Flying Angel House' is a pleasant, unpretentious building in a street running parallel to the magnificent beach a quarter of a mile away; it is some five miles from the docks. It has a comfortably furnished lounge with a highly polished floor, television, supplies of books, newspapers and magazines, a table tennis table and a pool table. Seafarers come to relax there, and many leave their belongings for safe keeping while they go to the beach. Many telephone home from the house. There are no organised shop or canteen facilities, but no seafarer fails to find refreshment in this lovely welcoming house, which is not only Frank and Betty Snedker's home but also a home-away-from-home to many people of many nations.

It has been the writer's privilege to see this loving, practical, sensible and caring couple at work on many occasions. They have faced, and come to terms with, the conditions of their environment. They complement each other most effectively. They are friends to many seafarers. The light and life of the Risen Lord shines in and through them.

Dubai
Ministry to Seafarers in the Gulf

Dubai is situated 25° North of the Equator in the Arabian Gulf. It is the major port of the United Arab Emirates, which lie between Oman to the East and Qatar to the West, with the vast territories of Saudi Arabia in the hinterland to the South and West. To the North, on the opposite shore of the Gulf, is Iran.

The development of port facilities in the United Arab Emirates after the steep increases in oil prices in 1973 and 1974 was phenomenal. In 1975, when the writer made the first of seven visits to the Gulf, Port Rashid (the port of Dubai) had some 20 berths in operation, with a similar number under construction, and a massive dry dock complex, with one dock capable of handling ships of up to 1 million deadweight tons, was also being built. In the years since then the development has been rapid and comprehensive. All the facilities have been upgraded, a well-equipped container terminal has been established and is flourishing, the cranes, wharves and warehouses are of excellent quality, the port is very tidy, and the ships turn round quickly. The dry docks worked to capacity on repairs to ships damaged in the Iran–Iraq War. In 1976 work started on the construction of a new port at Jebel Ali, 22 miles West of Dubai. 70 deep-water berths were planned for this breathtakingly vast and imaginative project, the total cost of which was expected to be in the region of £800 million. By 1982 the port, which had been quite literally scooped out of the desert, was operational, and by 1986 it was handling 3 million tons of petroleum, 3 million tons of general cargo, and a substantial and growing number of containers. It is the largest man-made harbour in the world, and its facilities are most impressive. In addition to Dubai and Jebel Ali, there are other major port facilities, including Abu Dhabi to the West and Sharjah to the East, in the United Arab Emirates.

During this time of remarkable growth and expansion in trade, commerce, shipping and port development in the United Arab Emirates, a number of Christian people were very active in seeking to establish the presence of the Church and a ministry to seafarers. In 1970 the Ruler of Dubai, Sheikh Rashid, made land available to the expatriate community for the building of a church, which they dedicated to the Holy Trinity. A non-denominational chaplaincy was established, a chaplaincy house was built with the aid of a loan from The Missions to Seamen, and The Missions to Seamen appointed a retired chaplain, Canon Haydn Parry, to pioneer the ministry. He was succeeded in 1972 by The Revd. Philip Sturdy, who in the six years he spent there not only ministered to the large and growing expatriate community but also gave strong support to the establishment of a seafarers' centre. His contribution was vital. He familiarised himself with the working of the port, got to know the people involved in its operation, visited the ships, promoted the concept of a seafarers' centre, and kept the Ruler informed of his work.

There were some fine people working in the port of Dubai who were also members of Holy Trinity Church and had been to sea themselves or had had long experience of the shipping industry. They had seen the Church's ministry to seafarers at first hand in different parts of the world, and were eager to play their part in establishing a seafarers' centre. Among them were Captain Arthur Jarman (the Port Manager), Captain Ian Butcher (the Assistant Port Manager) and Mr. George Chapman (Chairman of Dubai Port Services). The Ruler's Chief Financial Advisor, Mr. Bill Duff, and his Advisor for the Dubai Police Force, Mr. Jack Briggs, gave invaluable advice and assistance.

In December 1975 the writer visited Dubai and had a number of informative and important meetings with people interested in establishing a seafarers' centre, and with the committee of the Chaplaincy of Dubai and Sharjah, which governs the affairs of Holy Trinity Church. As a result of these meetings he, George Chapman, Bill Duff and Philip Sturdy sought and were granted an interview with the Ruler, Sheikh Rashid. At the end of this momentous meeting, in the course of which the Ruler was briefed about the nature and work of seafarers' centres all over the world, and shown photographs of some of them, the Ruler indicated that he would be happy to see a seafarers' centre established in Dubai, and would make available a building for this purpose. To say that there was great rejoicing would be an understatement!

A steering committee for the project was formed and a Statement of Intent was drawn up. The centre would be called the Dubai International Seafarers' Centre. Its aim and object would be 'the physical, spiritual and moral welfare of seafarers of all nations, races, creeds and backgrounds, irrespective of rank'.[5] Responsibility for its finances and administration would be assumed by a committee of management. A Constitution would be drawn up. The Missions to Seamen would appoint a suitably experienced person or persons to carry out the pastoral ministry of ship visting, hospital visiting and individual counselling. It was hoped that the ministry might be provided on an inter-confessional basis.

In May 1976 the Ruler made available a building right

outside the main gate of Port Rashid. Situated in a walled compound 130 yards long and 65 yards across, the two storey building was eminently suitable for a seafarers' centre. At the end of that month Captain Henry Severs, a recently retired Master Mariner, arrived to serve as Lay Assistant for The Missions to Seamen, to take charge of the day to day running of the Centre, and to co-ordinate fund-raising activities. He did a splendid job. Funds were raised locally and in the United Kingdom. The Chairman of P & O, Lord Inchcape, provided and personally hosted a magnificent luncheon in London which raised £25,000. The building was converted into a well-equipped seafarers' centre. A swimming pool was built. Two buses were purchased to transport seafarers to the Centre from their ships and back again—a much appreciated service in such a hot place. A shop, restaurant, indoor and outdoor recreational facilities, lounge, quiet room, thrift shop and other amenities were gradually added. In 1978 a full-time manager, a retired Indian Air Force officer, Wing Commander E. C. John, was appointed, and in 1980 The Missions to Seamen was able to appoint its chaplain to full-time ministry among seafarers when the Chaplaincy of Dubai and Sharjah felt that the tremendous increase in the work of the chaplaincy required the services of a chaplain on a full-time basis. Right from the outset the Dubai International Seafarers' Centre proved popular with seafarers, whose attendance has ranged between 1000 and 2000 every month.

The decision of The Missions to Seamen to put the chaplaincy to seafarers in Dubai on a full-time basis made it possible for successive chaplains to devote time to establishing maritime ministry on a wider basis throughout the United Arab Emirates. In 1986 a superb seafarers' centre was established in the new port of Jebel Ali through the initiative of two key people in the port, Captains Ralph Abbott and George Biro, and with the advice and support of the chaplains. The centre is within the dock complex, and is served by a bus which tours all the berths at regular intervals to pick up seafarers. It has all the facilities a seafarers' centre in a hot country needs—a shop, restaurant, canteen, telephones, currency exchange, indoor recreational amenities, and blissfully effective air-conditioning. It is a tribute to the work and witness of successive chaplains of The Missions to Seamen in Dubai that the authorities in Jebel Ali were keen that they should be closely involved in the operation of their seafarers' centre.

At the same time that the Dubai International Seafarers' Centre was being established, the Norwegian Seamen's Mission also built a centre in Dubai on land made available by the Ruler. It opened in 1976, and is a most attractive building, with two chaplaincy residences and club premises all designed in typical Norwegian style. It has an outdoor games area and a beautiful swimming pool. It serves both Scandinavian seafarers and the Scandinavian expatriate community.

In 1976, after his first visit to the Centre, the writer reported that 'the chaplains work in a most interesting way. One remains based in Dubai, while the other spends short times at sea on Scandinavian ships in the Gulf area. The relatively short distances between ports and the amount of congestion linked with long waiting periods outside ports makes this a most imaginative and valuable method of being alongside seafarers.' Sadly the long-running Gulf War has forced the suspension of this ministry for the time being. In 1987 some 500 Scandinavian seafarers visited the centre, and altogether nearly 10,000 Scandinavians made use of its facilities. All who call there are made most welcome.

In Dubai in 1988 those involved in maritime ministry were constantly faced with the traumas of the Gulf War. Distressed and injured seafarers whose ships had been attacked were part of the daily scene. The ships being repaired in the dry docks were a grim reminder of the horrific nature of modern warfare. Counselling survivors, comforting the injured, burying the dead, writing to bereaved families, and praying passionately for an end to fighting and bloodshed, were all part of a day's routine ministry.

Sarnia
A Mobile Ministry
An Anglican initiative

Sarnia is situated at the heart of the Great Lakes waterways of North America, 43° North of the Equator. It lies on the East bank of the Northern end of the St. Clair River, which links

Lake Huron in the North with Lake St. Clair, the Detroit River
and Lake Erie in the South, and forms the border between
Canada and the United States of America.

The St. Clair River is a vital link in the overall network of
communications in the Great Lakes. All vessels proceeding
from the Atlantic Ocean up the St. Lawrence River, through
the St. Lawrence Seaway, up the eight massive locks of the
Welland Canal, through Lake Erie, on their way to Lakes
Huron, Michigan and Superior, must navigate its 30 mile
length. Some 15,000 ships pass through it in the nine months
of the year when the Great Lakes are free of ice. They include
both ocean-going vessels of up to 30,000 deadweight tons
and 'lakers', strikingly distinctive ships specially built for the
unique navigation conditions of the freshwater Great Lakes in
which they operate exclusively.

Of the 14,750 ships which passed through the St. Clair River
in 1979, 4598 made stops at berths along the East (Canadian)
bank for cargo or bunkering purposes. 1690 berthed to deal
with cargo, and 2908 to bunker. Altogether there are 19 berths
along the East bank, spread out over a distance of 24 miles.
The ships spend between 2 and 14 hours at the berths, many of
which have very few shoreside facilities for seafarers and are
located a long way from shops, telephones or centres of
population.

In the late 1970's the chaplain of The Missions to Seamen in
Toronto, The Revd. David Mulholland, made a trip on a
'laker' in order to familiarise himself with the particular
conditions in which seafarers on these ships live and work.
Afterwards he initiated discussions in Sarnia with local clergy,
people involved in shipping, business men, and ultimately the
Anglican Diocese of Huron, to see whether it was feasible to
provide a ministry to the tens of thousands of seafarers whose
ships berthed, albeit briefly, along the River each year.

It was clear that the unusual conditions would require an
unusual ministry. Since the ships spent no more than a few
hours alongside it was essential that any chaplain, lay or
ordained, should be free to visit as soon as possible after they
berthed. Since the berths were spread over a distance of 24
miles, and were so well used, it was important that the chaplain
should be able to move quickly from berth to berth. And since
there were so few basic amenities for seafarers at some of the

berths, it was important that the chaplain should be able to cater for the most urgent needs. A mobile seafarers' centre, like the one already in use in Toronto, which could be driven from berth to berth and be parked without causing inconvenience, seemed to be the answer.

In 1981 the Diocese of Huron took the step of faith of accepting responsibility for establishing a mobile ministry on the St. Clair River, and The Revd. Stephen Gilbert was appointed as the first full-time chaplain. Stephen began his ministry in 1982, and an intensive programme of fund-raising to finance the whole operation was undertaken. A most generous grant of $46,500 from the International Transport Workers Federation made it possible to go ahead with the ordering and fitting out of a specially designed mobile seafarers' centre.

In October 1982 'Angie', as the centre came to be known because of the Flying Angel logo of The Missions to Seamen which is prominently displayed on the front, rear and sides, was handed over and went into service immediately. Twenty-six feet long and eight feet wide, it runs on petrol or propane gas. It is most imaginatively laid out. Behind the driver's and front passenger's seat there is a lounge area, with fixed comfortable swivel seats where seafarers can sit and watch the television (which is placed on a ledge between the front seats, and can be worked on batteries or plugged into the vehicle's cigar lighter!), or make phone calls on the radio telephone just behind the driver's seat. The entry door is in the middle of the vehicle, and behind the door there is a table with 4 comfortable seats where light refreshments can be served. The vehicle is equipped with a fridge/freezer, microwave cooker, gas oven, coffee maker, stereo-cassette system, toilet, shower, wash-basin, and very efficient heating and lighting systems. It has a 110 volt generator, and is air-conditioned. It also has a fold-down bed where the chaplain can sleep if he is visiting a remote berth where a ship may be alongside for just a few hours at night. It is carpeted and curtained.

The heart of the chaplain's ministry on the St. Clair River is ship visiting. He finds out from the Canadian Coastguard Traffic Center or the Sarnia Shipping Agency when and where the ships are going to berth, and he gets himself and 'Angie' there. Right from the outset 'Angie' has been a welcome sight to seafarers, who come down from their ships and spend time making use of the various facilities or just talking to the chaplain. One seafarer was so grateful for a helpful and important conversation that he sent a donation of $1500 as a thank-offering.

In October 1984 Stephen Gilbert retired as chaplain and, after an anxious period when it seemed likely that the mobile ministry would not be able to continue for financial reasons, Herb Jackson took over in 1985. Aged 71, retired after careers in the Navy and with an oil company, a Lay Reader in the Anglican Church, a member of the Board of The Missions to Seamen in Sarnia, and living in a house overlooking the St. Clair River, he offered to carry on the ministry without a salary. Since taking over he has visited an average of 25 ships per month with 'Angie'. He and his wife Terais (who died recently after a long illness, and will be greatly missed by the seafarers) often spent up to 12 hours alongside a ship. Some 200 seafarers a month visit 'Angie'. Herb's 'log' records ship visits, sight-seeing tours, shopping visits, transporting sick seafarers to hospital, provision of meals, and other services. The seafarers love him. The 'lakers' sound their sirens as they pass his house, and when 'Angie' is parked alongside a ship the chef often sends down a meal on a tray.

'Angie' is a place for relaxation, fellowship and worship. It is a home from home for people who are far from home and friends. It is equipped to provide a comprehensive service. It is a much-needed transport facility, and 'it helps to involve the local community in general and to arouse an awareness of the Society's work by promoting and displaying what The Missions to Seamen is undertaking locally'.[6]

Center for Seafarers' Rights, New York
The Center for Seafarers' Rights is a division of the Seamen's Church Institute of New York and New Jersey.

The Seamen's Church Institute of New York and New Jersey is an ecumenical centre affiliated with the Episcopal Church of the United States of America and is linked on a voluntary basis with the world-wide organisation of the Anglican Church, The

Missions to Seamen. Its Director, The Revd. Dr. James Whittemore, is the current chairman of the Standing Committee of the International Christian Maritime Association. It was founded in 1834 and has a long and distinguished history of promoting and actively campaigning for just treatment for seafarers of all races, ranks and creeds.

In the second half of the nineteenth century the Institute took on the thieves, crimps, unscrupulous and crooked boarding-house keepers and others who were amassing fortunes from the exploitation of the many seafarers from overseas in the port of New York. In 1898 a member of its Board, Mr. J. Augustus Johnson, established the Seamen's Branch of the Legal Aid Society and the then Director, Dr. Archibald Mansfield, worked closely with him to promote national legislation which would guarantee the basic rights of all seafarers. The Institute took up all kinds of cases on behalf of seafarers, including wages and contracts disputes, creditors' claims and imprisonment for desertion. It successfully campaigned for legislation in the United States for the protection of the employment and rights of seafarers.

Towards the end of the 1970's it became apparent to the present director of the Institute that the element of unjust treatment of seafarers, which has always been present in one form or another throughout maritime history, was manifesting itself in new and disturbing ways. There was a growing trend to register ships under flags of convenience and thereby effectively abrogate a measure of responsibility and obligation. There was a significant rise in ship losses. There was a steady decline in the number of seafarers from developed countries and a rapid increase in the number of seafarers from developing countries. The cruise ship industry was booming, and there were disturbing reports of the conditions in which some seafarers on some of these ships were serving. In 1980 the Institute appointed The Revd. Paul Chapman to establish a specialised ministry among seafarers experiencing unjust treatment and abuse of their rights as human beings.

Paul Chapman had been associated with the Civil Rights leader, the late Dr. Martin Luther King, and his project was entitled 'Human Rights for Seafarers'. In 1981 he was invited to address the Fourth Plenary Conference of the International Christian Maritime Association about his new work. He spoke

powerfully and movingly, and the conference pledged its full
support for what he was doing.

Later that year the project became 'The Center for Seafarers'
Rights'. It aimed to:

(i)   gather data on cases of unjust treatment, exploitation and
      the abuse of the dignity and value as human beings of
      seafarers,

(ii) work towards enabling the Seamen's Church Institute of
      New York and New Jersey to meet the needs of such
      seafarers, employing legal action and prompting legis-
      lative measures as necessary,

(iii) promote greater accountability among the owners of all
      ships entering United States' waters,

(iv) provide an advocacy service for seafarers experiencing
      unjust treatment,

(v)   press for the implementation of Port State Control regu-
      lations, and for a requirement that observance of basic
      human rights for seafarers be mandatory, and

(vi) examine the situation of seafarers today in the light of
      modern human rights standards and press for the resol-
      ution of problems of this nature on a national and inter-
      national basis.

Since its formal establishment as a division of the Seamen's
Church Institute of New York and New Jersey the Center for
Seafarers' Rights has made a great impact on the shipping
scene in North America and beyond. It has awakened the
consciences of a number of unscrupulous ship operators. It has
been diligent and meticulous in collecting, checking, correlat-
ing and sharing information concerning unjust treatment of
seafarers. It has worked with the authorities of the countries
involved to produce and distribute straightforward accurate
booklets advising seafarers of their rights on ships registered
under certain flag of convenience registries. It has sent representatives to attend and address national and international
conferences of seafarers' chaplains and other organisations
involved with seafaring. It has provided a free legal advice
service for seafarers who have been unjustly treated. It has
developed a network of marine lawyers in North America and
some other countries who are prepared to advise, assist and act
in cases of unjust or illegal treatment of seafarers. In 1984 it

organised a conference in Miami to draw attention to the plight of some seafarers serving on cruise vessels sailing out of that port. Between 1985 and 1987 it was instrumental in organising a successful campaign in the United States of America for the ratification of the International Labour Office Convention 147 'concerning minimum standards in merchant ships' and Port State Control; a conference it sponsored in New York in 1986 proved to be crucial to the success of the campaign. In December 1987 its representatives at the International Christian Maritime Association-sponsored Manning Agents Conference held in Manila were closely involved in drawing up a unanimously agreed Code of Good Practice for Manning Agents. It has fought for, and often been successful in obtaining compensation for, seafarers who have been injured at sea or on board ship and have experienced difficulty in getting satisfactory redress. Currently it is taking on an average of 250 new cases a year, together with about 25 referred from overseas. Paul Chapman writes a regular 'Know Your Rights' column in the bi-monthly magazine 'The Sea', published by The Missions to Seamen. Its work is held in respect, admiration and affection by thousands of grateful seafarers all over the world—and with undisguised hostility by many unscrupulous ship operators.

It is important to be clear that this is no trouble-seeking organisation. Paul Chapman and his colleagues are at pains to point out that they are dealing with a minority of shipowners and ship operators. 'While the majority of merchant ships are well operated and provide decent employment for their workers, on some ships there are problems. The Center receives hundreds of requests for help from individual seafarers every year.'[7] They work in happy collaboration with any organisations promoting the well-being of seafarers, complementing their work rather than competing with it. The Center provides an invaluable service to seafarers, seafarers' chaplains and the industry as a whole.

The Center for Seafarers' Rights has its offices in the temporary premises of the Seamen's Church Institute at 50 Broadway, Lower Manhattan, New York. Paul Chapman co-ordinates the work of a team of four people, which includes Jim Lafferty and Mike Smith (Marine Lawyers) and Brother Pedro of Taizé, who is a fine linguist and the point of contact for the seafarers.

Sullom Voe
An initiative of the British Sailors' Society

Sullom Voe is at the Northern end of the largest of the Shetland Islands, which are situated 200 miles to the North East of Scotland. It lies 60° North of the Equator, and 6° South of the Arctic Circle.

First impressions of Shetland are often of the barren landscape, the absence of trees, the large number of sheep, the sparseness of population and the miserable weather—though on a bright sunny day the islands have a striking beauty. In 1662 Captain John Smith wrote that 'the coldest weather is by reason of great winds in the winter quarter, the wind blowing so violent that no ship dare look on the North coast',[8] and it has been said that Shetland has nine months of winter and three months of bad weather!—though this is an exaggeration. The almost total absence of trees is due in part to the depredations of the sheep, which devoured the dwarf birch and willow which once grew there, and in part to the climate, which is not favourable to afforestation. The barrenness of the landscape is due mainly to the salt in the air from the autumn gales which can blight every green thing overnight.

The islands remained largely undeveloped until 1971, when substantial and marketable reserves of oil and natural gas were discovered about 100 miles to the East. At that time Sullom Voe, a deepwater inlet 28 miles North of Lerwick (the main centre of population of the islands), was virtually unheard of (except by World War II servicemen) outside Shetland. The land to the East of the Voe (which means inlet) was a peat bog. Just ten years later Europe's largest oil and liquefied gas terminal was officially opened there by Queen Elizabeth The Second. It had cost more than £15,000 million to extract the oil and gas and lay the pipelines to bring them ashore, and the terminal itself had cost a further £1175 million.

The planning and construction of the terminal followed an ideal pattern for such projects. In 1975 the newly-formed Shetland Islands Council (which replaced the former Zetland County Council, and represents the interests of the 23,000 inhabitants of the islands), and the oil industry (which was represented by Shell and BP as leaders respectively of the Brent and Ninian pipeline groups, and by B.P. as the terminal

Constructor), joined together to form the Sullom Voe Association, whose role was to provide a forum for discussion between the two parties and to co-ordinate the development and operation of the terminal. The terminal and necessary ancillary services, like housing, schools, sewage, airport etc., have been successfully absorbed into the island's life with a minimum of fuss and environmental disturbance. Pollution from the terminal is virtually nil, and penalties for offences against the strict regulations in operation are severe.

In November 1978 the first oil was piped ashore and the first shipment of it sent out. In 1979 141 million barrels of oil (19 million metric tons) were shipped out, and in 1986 the figure was 418 million barrels (55 million metric tons). In April 1981 the first gas was piped ashore, and in May 1982 the first shipment of Liquefied Petroleum Gas was made. In 1986 one and a half million tons of Liquefied Petroleum Gas (propane and butane) were piped ashore. In 1981 the total number of ships calling was 432 (all of them oil tankers), and in 1986 the figure was 766 (654 oil tankers and 112 gas carriers). There is a minimum depth of 60 feet alongside the four jetties.

Side by side with the planning and development of the terminal and its infrastructure there was an awareness in the Churches and among the partners of the Sullom Voe Association that appropriate provision must be made for the needs of the many seafarers whose ships would be berthed in this remote port. The British Sailors' Society, with strong support financially and in other ways from the oil companies, the Shetland Islands Council, the Merchant Navy Welfare Board and the International Transport Workers Federation, planned and built a splendid seafarers' centre one mile from the nearest jetty on land donated by Mr. Berti Johnson, a Shetlander. It opened in July 1981, a few weeks after the official opening of the terminal.

The Sullom Voe Seafarers' Centre, in which the British Sailors' Society invited the Apostleship of the Sea and The Missions to Seamen to be partners in the ministry, is a fine example of how a seafarers' centre in such a remote place should be planned. It is ideally situated as close as practicable to the jetties it serves. It provides all the amenities a seafarer whose ship is in port for no more than 24 hours can reasonably expect to find; these include a canteen where light meals are served throughout the day, a bar, a shop, T.V. and video, books and magazines to take on board, currency exchange facilities, sale of postage stamps, telephones, indoor games (including a full size snooker table, pool table and darts), and a quiet room/chapel. It has a minibus which transports seafarers between their ships and the centre at regular intervals free of charge.

It is very well used. Almost a thousand seafarers a month use its facilities, some 700 being brought in and taken back in the minibus. The shop, canteen, bar and telephones are much in demand, and an average of 800 international telephone calls are made by seafarers each month. There is an excellent atmosphere, which is enhanced by the presence of a number of terminal officials and employees who complement the welcome and service provided by the two full-time and four part-time members of staff. There is residential accommodation at the centre for a permanent member of the management staff, and the Shetland Islands Council has made available a very pleasant council house for occupation by a member of staff.

The writer has made two visits to the Centre. On each occasion it has been a hive of activity. The welcome offered to all was friendly, open, natural and spontaneous. It is a fine centre. It illustrates yet again the wonderful work Christians are doing all over the world among the seafarers of the world.

Dar es Salaam
An Anglican Initiative—an Inter-confessional Partnership—
in a Developing Country

Dar es Salaam, the capital of Tanzania, is situated on the East coast of Africa, 7° South of the Equator. Its busy and attractive harbour is one of the glories of the Indian Ocean.

The Anglican Missions to Seamen commenced its ministry to seafarers in Dar es Salaam in 1950, and a really excellent pioneering job was done by The Revd. John Rowlands. He established the ministry and saw the first and major stage of the building of a fine seafarers' centre completed. He was succeeded in 1961 by The Revd. John Taylor, who in the twelve years he was there built on the soundly-laid foundations and established a thriving and superbly equipped centre. He became Archdeacon of Dar es Salaam and Vicar General of the diocese, and combined a busy and much appreciated ministry among seafarers with a responsible position in the local Church. Both of these fine priests owed much to the vision, dedication and energy of their wives.

At the time when The Missions to Seamen was becoming established in Dar es Salaam, the movement among European-administered colonies in Africa towards seeking and obtaining independence was gathering momentum, and Tanganyika became independent in 1961. It retained its formal links with Kenya and Uganda with the formation of the East African Community, but this broke up in acrimony in 1977–78.

When the writer made his first visit to Tanzania in 1976 the country had embarked on a programme of left-wing Socialism under the idealistic leadership of the Roman Catholic President, Julius Nyerere. Close ties had been established with the People's Republic of China, the economy was in difficulties, many commodities were in short supply, strict foreign exchange regulations were in force, poverty was widespread, and new and irksome regulations affecting daily life had been introduced. There was only one official political party and a single trade union. In subsequent visits in 1979, 1982 and early 1984 the situation appeared to have changed very little, but in 1987 the economy had improved and a more positive and optimistic atmosphere was apparent.

It was against the background of a nation emerging from colonial status to independence and a distinctive identity of its own that The Missions to Seamen established its ministry in Dar es Salaam. Right from the beginning it has enjoyed the wholehearted backing of the Anglican Church in Tanzania. President Julius Nyerere accepted the position of President of the Society's work in Tanzania, and has continued to take a keen interest in the work. And in recent years it has had the strong support of the Roman Catholic Church under the leadership of Cardinal Laurian Rugambwa, who appointed a priest of the Society of Missionaries of Africa (the White Fathers), Father Georges Loire, to work in partnership with the Anglican port chaplain from the seafarers' centre of The Missions to Seamen. It has proved to be a very happy arrangement.

The port of Dar es Salaam is busy. Its eleven berths are well used, and an excellent container terminal has been built. It is tidy, and there is a purposeful air about its workings. In 1986, 632 overseas registered vessels and 250 Tanzanian coasters used the port, and these figures do not take into account the dhows, lighters, warships and other vessels which called. Because of the nature of much of the cargo they handle many ships (but not the container vessels) spend several days in port, and this affords a golden opportunity to the chaplains to get to know the seafarers on board and to take them on an occasional safari trip to the beautiful National Parks.

The seafarers' centre of The Missions to Seamen is ideally located opposite one of the main gates of the port. It is magnificent—imaginatively designed, well built, well equipped and beautifully maintained. Its amenities include a lovely chapel, comfortable lounge, bar, restaurant, shop, swimming pool, children's play area, full size soccer pitch, outdoor lounge area, tennis court, large putting course, good offices for the chaplains, carefully tended flower gardens, and accommodation for the chaplains and Warden. The staff look after the whole complex very efficiently, and the immaculate condition of the chapel—its highly polished floor and furniture, and the regular supply of fresh flowers—reflects the priorities of the Warden, David Hodgson. The chapel is the powerhouse of the whole operation. The centre is extremely well used, some 5000 visits a month being made by seafarers.

The chaplaincy team is international and inter-confessional. The Senior Chaplain is The Right Reverend John Watanabe, who was formerly Bishop of Hokkaido and Primate of the Nippon Sei Ko Kai (the Anglican Church of Japan). A former seafarer—he was a naval cadet in Japan when the atomic bomb was dropped on nearby Hiroshima in 1945, and the deep impression this made on him ultimately brought him to faith in Jesus Christ—he resigned early from his diocese in order to become a chaplain with The Missions to Seamen. He was trained for the ministry among seafarers by a Chinese chaplain in Melbourne in Australia. Since his arrival in Dar Es Salaam, in September 1987, he has made a great impact both among seafarers and in the Anglican Church in Tanzania. He is learning Swahili, and has conducted Confirmation services in that language whenever the Diocesan Bishop (himself a former chaplain of The Missions to Seamen in Dar es Salaam and Maputo) has invited him to do so. He and his wife Ruth are already much loved and respected. The Roman Catholic chaplain, Father Georges Loire, has also made a great impression among seafarers and shoreside people; he is quiet, gentle, firm and co-operative, with a delightful sense of humour, and he is fully committed to inter-confessional collaboration. The Warden, David Hodgson, has been responsible for lifting the seafarers' centre to the high standard at which it currently operates. An Anglican Lay Reader, unmarried, a former Chief Steward at sea for many years, and a lay member of the Franciscan Order, David simply lives for his work. He personally supervises the daily running of the centre, and the inspiration for the lively ecumenical Sunday evening worship came from him. There is a daily staff meeting to discuss and plan the work.

The Sunday chapel services are exciting. In the morning there is a well-attended Anglican celebration of Holy Communion. Seafarers and shore people attend, and there is a good choir of young Tanzanians. A Roman Catholic Mass follows, and this also is well attended. In the evening the choir members return for the ecumenical service. The singing is inspiring, and the congregation is truly international.

The committee of management of the seafarers' centre is made up almost entirely of Tanzanians. The seafarers' centre in Dar es Salaam is both the outreach of the Church in Tanzania and also an international and interconfessional partnership in ministry.

Laus Deo!

Notes

1. Information supplied by The Revd. Bernard Krug, General Secretary of The International Christian Maritime Association which publishes regularly a Directory of Seafarers' entres and Agencies.
2. Report of the visit of The General Secretary of The Missions to Seamen, The Revd. W. J. D. Down, to Napier on November 19th 1984 p. 2.
3. Ibid. p. 4.
4. Report of the Senior Chaplain of The Missions to Seamen in Hong Kong, The Revd. Geoffrey Shrives, to the General Secretary of The Missions to Seamen, dated January 1970.

5. Statement of Intent for the establishment of the Dubai International Seafarers' Centre, December 8th 1975. This statement was slightly amended in November 1976, though this clause was left unaltered.

6. The Revd. Stephen Gilbert, chaplain of The Missions to Seamen in Sarnia 1982–1984.

7. Resource Bulletin for the Port State Control Conference held in New York April 2–4 1986 published by the Seamen's Church Institute—Center for Seafarers' Rights, p. 14.

8. 'The islands and their people', by Dr. Jonathan Wills, which is part of a booklet entitled 'Sullom Voe Terminal Shetland', published by External Relations, BP Petroleum Development Limited, in November 1986. Dr. Wills, who quotes the extract from Captain Smith's records, is a journalist with 'The Shetland Times'.

IX On Course Together

'There is one body and one spirit, as there is also one hope
held out in God's call to you: one Lord, one faith, one
baptism; one God and Father of all, who is over all and
through all and in all.'
St. Paul's Epistle to the Ephesians, Chapter 4, verses 4 to 6.

It is clear from what has already been written that in the sphere
of maritime ministry the Christian denominational and non-
denominational organisations see their future in terms of
inter-confessional collaboration and partnership with each
other. In their witness and service to the seafarers of the world
they are on course together. It is also clear that if they are to
make their full contribution to the life, work and witness of the
Church as a whole their further development and future
collaboration must not only not be inhibited by undue con-
straints but also actively fostered and encouraged by the
Churches.

But the way ahead is not going to be easy. Maritime ministry
is only one small (though significant) part of the Church's
outreach to the world, and the individual Churches are facing
formidable obstacles and challenges, as well as receiving
heartening encouragement, as they seek to draw closer to each
other. A general understanding of where the Churches currently stand in relation to each other is essential if the full
dynamic potential of maritime ministry in the ecumenical
movement is to be understood and fulfilled.

Inter-Church Relations Today

It is encouraging to see how the Churches have drawn closer to
each other in the twentieth century, and a brief recapitulation

of some of the significant stages in this process may be helpful in formulating an assessment of the current situation.

As has already been noted* the ecumenical movement had its origins in the Reformed Churches in the eighteenth century, when the Evangelical Revivals which took place in a number of countries brought together Christians of different allegiances in programmes of social reform which transcended doctrinal divisions, and when the work of the Bible Societies proved to be a uniting factor. At the beginning of the twentieth century the Edinburgh Conference of 1910, which brought together 1200 delegates from 160 missionary societies and was notable for the beginning of a concerted effort to introduce a programme of world evangelism, marked an historic step forward in ecumenical relations. So too did the unequivocal call to all Communions, by the Bishops of the Anglican Communion at the 1920 Lambeth Conference, to unite in seeking to recover and manifest to the world the unity of the Body of Christ for which He prayed.

Another major advance came in 1938 with the establishment of the World Council of Churches, though because of the advent of the Second World War its first plenary session was not held until 1948. In 1947 the Church of South India was founded. It brought together the Anglicans, Methodists and the South India United Church (which itself had brought together Presbyterians, Congregationalists and Dutch Reformed Christians), and marked a significant step forward in inter-Church relations.

In 1960 a historic meeting took place in Rome between Pope John XXIII and the Anglican Archbishop of Canterbury, Geoffrey Fisher. 'When John and Geoffrey, two elderly ecclesiastics, had sat down in the Pope's study, and had exchanged more formal greetings, the Pope read to the Archbishop a passage in English which referred to the time when "our separated brethren should return to the Mother Church" . . . At that point Fisher interrupted: "Your Holiness, not return." The Pope looked puzzled and asked, "Not return? Why not?", to which Fisher replied: "None of us can go backwards. We are each now running on parallel courses; we are looking forward, until, in God's good time, our courses approximate

* See Chapters Three and Five.

and meet." The Pope paused to think about this and then said, "You are right""[1] Also in 1960 Pope John XXIII instituted the Second Vatican Council, which met in four very long sessions every year between 1962 and 1965. It was described as 'the most important ecclesiastical event of this century, not just for Roman Catholics but for all Christians'.[2] From this point onwards the Roman Catholic Church committed itelf to the path of inter-confessional collaboration.

In 1969 the International Christian Maritime Association came into being. In 1970 the Church of North India was established; it brought together Anglicans, Congregationalists, Presbyterians, Methodists, Baptists, the Church of the Brethren and the Disciples of Christ.[3] In 1982 Pope John Paul II made a historic visit to Canterbury Cathedral, where in a most moving service he was greeted and welcomed by the Archbishop of Canterbury, Robert Runcie.

In 1987 330 representatives from all the major Christian affiliations in Great Britain and Ireland came together at The Not Strangers but Pilgrims Conference held in Swanwick as part of the Inter-Church Process. They included Anglicans, Baptists, Congregationalists, Greek Orthodox, Lutherans, Methodists, Presbyterians, Roman Catholics, Russian Orthodox, Salvation Army and United Reformed Church delegates. They produced a remarkable, memorable and far-reaching declaration, which stated, inter alia, that:

'We now declare together our readiness to commit ourselves to each other under God. Our earnest desire is to become more fully, in his own time, the One Church of Christ, united in faith, communion, pastoral care and mission. Such unity is the gift of God . . . In the unity we seek we recognise that there will not be uniformity but legitimate diversity . . . It is our conviction that, as a matter of policy at all levels and in all places, our churches must now move from co-operation to clear commitment to each other, in search of the unity for which Christ prayed, and in common evangelism and service of the world . . . This is a new beginning. We set out on our further pilgrimage ready to take risks and determined not to be put off by "dismal stories" . . . Leaving behind painful memories and reaching out for what lies ahead, we press on towards the full reconciliation in Christ of all things in heaven and on earth, that God has promised in His Kingdom.'[4]

At the level of serious theological discussion official conversations on the issues which separate the Churches have been held and are being held between individual Churches.[5] Encouraging progress has been made and is being made. A substantial measure of doctrinal agreement has been reached in some of the conversations. Inter-communion between some Churches is a reality. The process is painstaking and slow, but the atmosphere and the inter-personal relationships are good, and the determination to move forward is strong.

At the level of decision-making in the Churches it is encouraging that cordial relations exist between the bishops and leaders of the various Churches in many places. The publication of 'Better Together, Christian partnership in a hurt City'[6] by David Sheppard, the Anglican Bishop of Liverpool, and his Roman Catholic counterpart, Archbishop Derek Worlock, is a symbol of the many bonds of respect, affection, trust and collaboration which have been forged between Christian leaders of different traditions in recent years. Similar relationships have been established and are being established among the clergy working at parish and chaplaincy level.

At the level of parochial and congregational life it is encouraging to observe the ways in which barriers are being broken down through participation in inter-Church activities such as the Week of Prayer for Christian Unity, joint community projects[7] and programmes like 'Not Strangers But Pilgrims'.[8] In his travels in many parts of the world in the last fourteen years the writer has become aware of a strong and growing desire for inter-communion and increased collaboration among many lay people and clergy of many Christian traditions in many parts of the world.

All of this is very satisfactory. But formidable hurdles remain, presenting challenges which must be tackled and overcome if the Churches are to draw closer together in their witness to the Living Lord.

Major doctrinal issues still separate the Churches. Decisions of the past can be difficult to change or re-interpret. Prejudice and bigotry die hard. Apathy and indifference hinder growth. In the Anglican Communion the ordination of women to the priesthood and now to the episcopate is presenting problems in the relationships between its members and in the Communion's relationships with some other major Churches. The relationship between the Churches and people of other faiths is still being worked out. The ever-present problems of poverty, hunger, famine, homelessness, injustice, abuse of human dignity and rights, exploitation and warfare demand the immediate attention of the Churches: they also afford a marvellous opportunity for common service, witness and action. Nobody should under-estimate the size and extent of these problems.

This brief and necessarily inadequate general sketch of where the Churches currently stand in relation to each other sets the ecumenical scene to which developments in maritime ministry over the past quarter of a century have much to contribute.

The Potential Contribution of the Churches' Maritime Ministry to the Life of the Church As a Whole

The contribution the maritime ministries of the Churches can make to the life of the Church as a whole can be identified from a study of what has been achieved in recent years in this specialised area of Christian service.

From the time of the inauguration of the Second Vatican Council in 1960, and more especially since the establishment of the International Christian Maritime Association in 1969, there has been a widespread and comprehensive breaking down of barriers between Christians ministering to seafarers. It can be seen at every level. Excellent relationships have been established between the hierarchies of the various denominational and non-denominational organisations, the clergy and lay staff work together very happily, and seafarers can see what has happened. Contrast the comment made in 1972 by a seafarer to a chaplain when he saw a chaplain of another denomination coming up his ship's gangway—'Oh, Padre, the opposition's here!'—with the comment of a seafarer in 1975 to a chaplain from a jointly-operated seafarers' centre whose colleague of another denomination had visited the ship the previous day—'Oh, Padre, I was talking to your mate yesterday.'

In 1969 the International Christian Maritime Association* was established. It brought together in a free association all the major Christian denominations and societies serving sea-farers, and its aim was to promote inter-confessional collabor-ation, enable it to take place, and speak with authority as the collective voice of its members. Its impact has been enormous and its influence is great. It has achieved wonders.

From the mid 1960's, and especially since the establishment of the International Christian Maritime Association, inter-confessional collaboration has been a fact and a reality in many ports of the world. In some early joint operations mistakes were made through over-enthusiasm, failure to think through all the implications of partnership, personal incom-patibilities and mistaken motivation. It soon became clear, however, that the blessing, support and active involvement of the appropriate bishops and Church leaders was vital if joint operations were to be established on a sound base, and this backing was willingly given. Inter-confessional collaboration has brought an enriching of their personal discipleship for many chaplains and lay people through their daily fellowship with Christians of other traditions, a better and deeper under-standing of other traditions, the creation of mutual accept-ance, and the possibility of speaking and acting together on important matters.

The advent of inter-confessional collaboration has led to the rationalisation and modernisation of long-established sea-farers' centres when a number of organisations have agreed to work together in partnership from one building. The question of the ownership of property when organisations of different ecclesiastical traditions come together to work in partnership has led to widespread acceptance of the principle that all parties are equal partners in the ministry and guests of the organisation which owns the building. When new seafarers' centres are to be jointly established—and a significant number have been built in many parts of the world in the last twenty

---

* Chapter Seven of this book is devoted in its entirety to a study and evaluation of the International Christian Maritime Association.

years—all the partners contribute finance and/or personnel, and often one organisation acts as Trustee on behalf of the others; in some cases the local Anglican and Roman Catholic Bishops act as joint Trustees.

Inter-confessional collaboration has added a new dimension to the traditionally international outlook of seafarers' chaplains and others involved in maritime ministry. Daily contact with seafarers from many countries, many cultures, many faiths, many ideologies—and no ideologies—gives seafarers' chaplains the highly unusual experience of welcoming representatives of the whole world into their centres every day. When their experience, knowledge and insights are shared with other Christians from all over the world engaged in similar ministries at regular regional and international conferences organised on an inter-confessional basis by the International Christian Maritime Association, it is immediately clear that a vast and invaluable reservoir of theological wisdom is available to the Churches.

Inter-confessional collaboration has also resulted in a significant number of the denominational organisations ministering to seafarers becoming more closely integrated into the life of their parent churches. The (Anglican) Missions to Seamen, which started its life as a voluntary missionary society of the Church of England with stations and representatives overseas, has more recently become the Anglican Communion's outreach to seafarers. The Anglican Communion has willingly accepted more and more responsibility for the pastoral and administrative oversight of its work through Liaison Bishops and Councils in the various Provinces, and the current nature of the Society's work was affirmed by the following unanimously adopted resolution of the 1988 Lambeth Conference of Bishops of the Anglican Communion:

'This Conference thanks God for the world-wide Missions to Seamen which began its work in 1856. It supports and endorses the remarkable way in which the Society has adapted its ministry to changed circumstances, acknowledging the fact that there is no part of the Church which has greater ecumenical involvement and experience; that it is deeply involved in dialogue with people of other faiths every day; and that through the Center for Seafarers' Rights, and through almost every member of staff, it is daily involved in issues of social justice. The Conference, encouraged by the appointment of Liaison Bishops throughout the Anglican Communion, accepts the Ministry and Mission of the Society as the Mission of the Church to all seafarers, regardless of creed, class or colour.'

In 1970 the Roman Catholic Church established the Pontifical Commission for the Pastoral Care of Migrant and Itinerant People in order to lend added support to the Apostleship of the Sea, its official outreach to seafarers, and to incorporate its experience and insights into the life of the Church. In the 1970's the German Seamen's Mission began to operate on an inter-confessional basis with other organisations, and its experience is already proving a stimulus to the Lutheran Church. The non-denominational British Sailors' Society shares its experience and insights gained from inter-confessional collaboration with the Free Churches. And in a remarkable piece of imaginative ecumenism the Roman Catholic Apostleship of the Sea, the non-denominational British Sailors Society, the Lutheran German Seamen's Mission and the Anglican Missions to Seamen transferred the ownership of the magnificent new seafarers' centre in Jakarta (which they had combined to plan, finance and build) to the Indonesian Communion of Churches, agreeing at the same time to collaborate with the Indonesian Communion of Churches and give them a measure of financial support.

In the sphere of maritime ministry the major issues facing the Church as a whole are being faced and tackled. The unjust treatment and exploitation of some seafarers is, and always has been, a cause of great concern to Christian maritime organisations. Current manifestations of the problem are dealt with daily by the Center for Seafarers' Rights in New York* and individual seafarers' chaplains around the world. Dialogue with people of other faiths takes place daily in maritime ministry. Ecumenism and inter-confessional collaboration are at the heart of this ministry—the various organisations pray together, plan together, work together and laugh together.

---

* See the section 'Center for Seafarers Rights' in Chapter Eight for details of the work of this specialist group.

Living ecumenism is the hallmark of this ministry. Inter-communion is the heartfelt longing of most Christians involved in this work, and frustration at the slowness of progress towards achieving it is very near the surface.

In the sphere of maritime ministry the Christian organisations have got their act together. We are on course together. We are ready to move forward together.

The Course Ahead

As the Christian organisations of the different ecclesiastical traditions involved in maritime ministry look ahead to the future, they will all be looking to strengthen the bonds which already unite them. Loyal to their Church disciplines, they will seek to draw closer to each other, to build on their already established commitment to each other, to work for the unity which is Our Lord Jesus Christ's will for His Church, and to present a united, effective, attractive and vibrant ministry to seafarers.

They will actively seek to share with the Churches their experience of inter-confessional collaboration, take a full part themselves in the life of the Churches, make the Churches aware of the value of their ministry, and encourage the Churches to accept that ministry to seafarers is the responsibility of the whole Church and not just of a few organisations and individuals.

They will surely follow the course of increasingly rationalising their resources, establishing new seafarers' centres together where these are necessary, up-dating their concept of ministry, and agonising over theological issues such as ecumenism, justice, and relations with people of other faiths.

They have already embarked on a thorough-going review of the work and future role of the International Christian Maritime Association, and this will be a continuing process. They are seeking to establish closer links with the Orthodox Churches, and great efforts will be made to achieve this. They are seeking greater involvement in the councils of the shipping world. They will continue to work closely with secular organisations concerned with the welfare of seafarers. They will continue to exercise a prophetic ministry and be the conscience of the industry.

They will need to monitor closely the changes constantly taking place in the shipping world in order to ensure that their ministry is relevant and appropriate. They will need to spare no effort to bring about a situation where the seafarers of the world are served by Christians from all over the world.

In the maritime world the Churches are on course together. God grant that this may always be so.

'O Lord God, when Thou givest to Thy servants to endeavour any great matter, grant us also to know that it is not the beginning but the continuing of the same unto the end, until it be thoroughly finished, which yieldeth the true glory; through him who for the finishing of thy work laid down his life, our Redeemer, Jesus Christ. Amen.'

A prayer of a famous sailor, Sir Francis Drake.

Notes

1. Adrian Hastings, 'A History of English Christianity 1920–1985', p. 523.
2. Ibid. p. 525.
3. The Oxford Dictionary of the Christian Church has the following description of the Church of North India:
   'The Church, inaugurated on 29 November 1970 by the union of six Christian bodies, viz. the Anglican Church of India, Pakistan and Ceylon in respect of 13 dioceses; the United Church of North India, itself a union of Congregationalists and Presbyterians dating from 1924; the circuits of the Methodist Church linked with Britain and Australia; the Baptists; the Church of the Brethren, which originated in Germany and was brought to India by American missionaries in 1895; and the Disciples of Christ', p. 981.
4. 'Not Strangers But Pilgrims', Report of the Swanwick Conference 31 August to 4 September 1987, published jointly by the British Council of Churches and the Catholic Truth Society for the Inter-Church Process, pp. 3 and 4.
5. The official inter-Church dialogues which are currently taking place include those of the Anglican-Roman Catholic International Commission (the first of which was set up in 1966 by the Common Declaration of Pope Paul VI and Archbishop Michael Ramsey, and published its final report in 1982; the second, which is still meeting, was set up following the visit of Pope John Paul II to Archbishop Robert Runcie at

Canterbury in 1982). Continuing discussions are taking place between the Anglican and Lutheran Churches, the Anglican and Orthodox Churches, the Roman Catholic Church and a number of other Churches, etc., etc..

6. 'Better Together', by David Sheppard and Derek Worlock, was published in 1988 by Hodder and Stoughton. Bishop Sheppard and Archbishop Worlock have served in their present positions in Liverpool since the mid 1970's, and they have worked closely together in happy partnership to encourage reconciliation, co-operation and the renewal of community life in Liverpool.

7. 'The Measure of Mission', the report of The Mission Theological Advisory Group of the Board for Mission and Unity of the General Synod of the Church of England and of the Partnership for World Mission, describes in some detail a number of projects illustrating community outreach in different parts of the world.

8. See Note 4. The Inter-Church Process in Great Britain and Ireland is a continuing programme of inter-Church joint discussion and action at all levels of the Churches involved, and the list of participating Churches and Associations is as follows:

African Methodist Episcopal Church
Afro-West Indian United Council of Churches
Baptist Union of Great Britain and Ireland
Baptist Union of Wales
Black Pastors' Conference
Calvary Church of God in Christ
Cherubim and Seraphim Council of Churches
Christian Brethren
Church in Wales
Church of England
Church of Scotland
Congregational Federation
Congregational Union of Scotland
Council of African and Afro-Caribbean Churches
Greek Orthodox Church
Independent Methodist Church
International Ministerial Council of Great Britain
Lutheran Council of Great Britain
Methodist Church
Moravian Church
New Testament Assembly
Old Baptist Union
Presbyterian Church of Wales
Roman Catholic Church in England and Wales
Roman Catholic Church in Scotland
Russian Orthodox Church
Salvation Army
Scottish Episcopalian Church
Shiloh United Church of Christ
Society of Friends

Union of Welsh Independents
Unitarian Church
United Free Church of Scotland
United Reformed Church
Wesleyan Holiness Church
West Indian Evangelical Alliance

It plans to implement agreed proposals for a 'New Ecumenical Instrument for Britain and Ireland' in 1990.

Bibliography

'Seamen's Missions: Their Origin and Early Growth', by Roald Kverndal. Published in 1986 by William Carey Library of Pasadena, California.

'The Church and the Sailor', by Peter Anson. Published in 1948 by the Catholic Book Club of London.

'At the Sign of the Flying Angel', by G. A. Gollock. Published in 1930 by Longmans, Green and Co. of London, New York and Toronto.

'The Ship: The Century before Steam', by Alan McGowan. Published by Her Majesty's Stationery Office, London, in 1980.

'The Sea Chaplains', by Gordon Taylor. Published in 1978 by the Oxford Illustrated Press.

'The Log of a Sky Pilot', by T. Stanley Treanor. Published in 1893 by the Religious Tract Society of London.

'Heroes of the Goodwin Sands', by T. Stanley Treanor. Published 1904 by the Religious Tract Society of London.

'Finding Men for Christ', by George F. Dempster. Published in 1935 by Hodder and Stoughton, Ltd., of London.

'Flying Angel', by L. A. G. Strong. Published in 1956 by Methuen and Company Ltd., of London.

'Fish and Ships', by Stanley Pritchard. Published by Mowbray of London and Oxford in 1980.

'Piracy Today', by Roger Villar. Published in 1985 by Conway Maritime Press of London.

'A History of English Christianity 1920–1985', by Adrian Hastings. Published in 1986 by Collins Fount Paperbacks.

'The Pelican History of the World', by J. M. Roberts. Published in 1980 by Pelican Books of Harmondsworth, England.

'The Oxford Companion to Ships and the Sea', edited by Peter Kemp. Published in 1976 by the Oxford University Press.

'The Story of P & O', by David Howarth and Stephen Howarth. Published in 1986 by Weidenfeld and Nicholson of London.

'Ocean Ships', by David Hornby (1986 Edition). Published in 1986 by Ian Allan Ltd. of Shepperton, Surrey.

'The Guinness Book of Ships and Shipping: Facts and Feats', Edited by Tom Hartman. Published in 1983 by Guinness Superlatives of Enfield, Middlesex.

'The Ship: The Revolution in Merchant Shipping 1950–1980', by Ewan Corlett. Published in 1981 by Her Majesty's Stationery Office.

'Ports of the World 1988', edited by Paul Cuny. Published by Lloyds of London Press.

'Atlas of the Oceans', edited by Alastair Couper. Published in 1983 by Times Books Limited of London.

'A History of Europe, from the beginning of the Eighteenth Century to 1937', by H. A. L. Fisher. Published by Eyre and Spottiswoode of London 1952.

'The McGraw-Hill Illustrated World History', edited by Esmond Wright and Kenneth M. Stampp. Published in 1964 by McGraw-Hill Publishing Company Limited of New York, Toronto and London.

'Maritime Manning Conference Manila 7–9 December 1987'— a report published by the International Christian Maritime Association.

'Seafarers' Survey: An analysis of a survey taken from 4525 seafarers in 59 ports', written by Bernard Krug and published by the International Christian Maritime Association in 1988.

'From Holystones to Gantry Cranes', a brief history of the Seamen's Church Institute of New York and New Jersey, published by the S.C.I. of New York and New Jersey, 1984.

'Larousse Encyclopaedia of Modern History', published by Paul Hamlyn of London, 1967.

'Journal of the "Seamen's Wives Association of the Philippines"', published by Salesiana Publishers Incorporated, Makati, Metro Manila, 1984.

'Not Strangers But Pilgrims'—the Report of the Swanwick Conference 31 August to 4 September 1987, published jointly by the British Council of Churches and the Catholic Truth Society for the Inter-Church Process.

'The Measure of Mission' (a report of the Mission Theological Advisory Group of the Board for Mission and Unity of the General Synod of the Church of England and of the Partnership for World Mission) published in 1987 by the Board for Mission and Unity of the Church of England and of the Partnership for World Mission.

Conference Reports of the International Christian Maritime Association:
Rotterdam, 1969
London, 1972
Elsinore, 1975
New York, 1978
Berlin, 1981

The Philippines, 1985
All published by the International Christian Maritime Association, of 81, Orwell Road, Felixstowe, IP11 7PY, England.
Conference reports of the Apostleship of the Sea:
Hong Kong 1977
Rome 1982
Mombasa 1987
All published by the Pontifical Commission for the Pastoral Care of Migrants and Itinerant People.

Articles

'Missions to Seamen', by Jan Ørner in the International Review of Mission, July 1971.
Captain Jan Ørner was Deputy Director of Inter-Church Aid, Refugee and World Service of the World Council of Churches, and Secretary of the International Christian Maritime Association.
'Where have we come from?' by Roald Kverndal. A paper delivered to the North American Maritime Ministries Conference held at Corpus Christi, Texas, in October 1985.
'Decline in the U.K. Registered Merchant Fleet'—Minutes of evidence submitted to the House of Commons Transport Committee by the British Motor Ship Owners Association and the British Maritime League. Published by Her Majesty's Stationery Office, 1987.
'The Future of the British Merchant Fleet'—General Council of British Shipping, London December 1987.
'The Marine Society—Historical Notes and Present Operations', The Marine Society, London 1988.
'Human Rights Violations at Sea—the tip of the iceberg', by Colin V. D. Smith, published by International Institute for Transportation and Ocean Policy Studies, Dalhousie University, Halifax, Nova Scotia, in 1987.
Many articles from 'Chart and Compass', the magazine of the British Sailors' Society.
Many articles from 'Flying Angel News', the quarterly newspaper of The Missions to Seamen.
Many articles from 'The Sea', a bi-monthly publication for seafarers published by The Missions to Seamen.
'John Williams Seven', published by London Missionary Society, 11 Carteret Street, London SW1.

Appendix A

CASUALTY RETURNS
ANNUAL SUMMARY
1986

(Ships of 500 tons gross and over)

The undermentioned report of Total Losses, including Constructive Total Losses, recorded during 1986 has been issued by The Institute of London Underwriters.

BY NATURE OF CASUALTY

Nature of Casualty	United Kingdom	Others	Total
Weather	—	40	40
Founderings and Abandonments	—	32	32
Strandings	—	23	23
Collisions	—	7	7
Contact	—	2	2
Fires and Explosions	—	38	38
Missing	—	2	2
Machinery, etc.	—	9	9
Other Casualties	—	3	3
Totals 1986	—	156	156
Total 1985	3	185	188
Totals 1984	—	214	214
Totals 1983	—	209	209
Totals 1982	4	232	236

BY NATIONALITY

NATIONALITY	1982 No.	1982 G.R.T.	1983 No.	1983 G.R.T.	1984 No.	1984 G.R.T.	1985 No.	1985 G.R.T.	1986 No.	1986 G.R.T.
Algeria	—	—	—	—	—	—	—	—	1	3,629
Angola	—	—	—	—	—	—	1	8,374	—	—
Argentina	—	—	2	2,775	1	12,443	1	2,122	1	3,210
Australia	1	1,160	—	—	—	—	—	—	2	21,588
Bahamas	—	—	1	7,692	3	24,211	1	769	—	—
Bangladesh	—	—	1	888	—	—	—	—	—	—
Belgium	2	5,096	—	—	1	1,593	—	—	—	—
Bermuda	—	—	1	1,599	2	6,465	—	—	—	—
Brazil	2	17,463	—	—	—	—	3	9,636	1	11,373
Cameroun	1	1,601	—	—	—	—	—	—	—	—
Canada	5	8,787	6	13,649	1	1,106	1	616	1	1,539
Cayman Islands	2	14,655	2	8,577	3	3,058	2	3,502	—	—
Chile	1	536	—	—	1	742	1	678	1	58,213
China	2	10,805	2	22,578	2	15,288	—	—	1	3,995
Colombia	—	—	—	—	3	20,600	—	—	—	—
Costa Rica	—	—	—	—	—	—	1	678	—	—
Cuba	1	9,390	2	3,500	10	—	3	20,173	1	11,072
Cyprus	16	76,767	5	21,864	—	43,171	11	42,285	15	104,929
Denmark	1	789	—	—	1	722	1	1,857	1	597
Dubai	1	1,007	—	—	1	500	—	—	—	—
Ecuador	—	—	—	—	1	619	1	1,969	1	1,432
Egypt	—	—	1	1,532	1	791	1	697	1	1,277
Faroe Islands	—	—	—	—	1	1,072	—	—	—	—
Finland	—	—	—	—	1	1,323	1	12,390	1	2,326

Country										
France	1	645	—	—	1	4,210	—	—	2	3,152
Gambia	—	—	—	—	1	703	—	—	—	—
Germany, East	1	1,539	—	—	2	21,739	—	—	2	9,972
Germany, West	1	1,514	2	4,981	2	2,299	2	4,597	—	—
Ghana	—	—	1	7,594	2	2,597	—	—	1	1,230
Gibraltar	—	—	—	—	—	—	—	23,855	—	—
Greece	43	343,597	30	329,370	30	349,623	11	177,342	15	197,953
Holland	3	4,006	—	—	1	1,719	—	—	1	3,970
Honduras	2	4,540	—	—	2	5,132	—	—	2	1,744
Hong Kong	—	—	—	—	—	—	5	9,024	2	92,631
Iceland	1	1,143	—	—	1	671	—	—	1	2,333
India	1	9,612	1	2,940	—	—	5	54,816	1	24,573
Indonesia	6	12,541	6	11,154	2	4,726	—	—	1	1,630
Iran	—	—	—	—	1	10,205	—	—	—	—
Iraq	1	3,135	—	—	—	—	—	—	—	—
Israel	5	5,019	—	—	—	—	—	—	—	—
Italy	—	28,448	3	15,519	3	15,613	8	10,696	4	5,586
Ivory Coast	3	—	—	—	—	—	1	8,553	—	—
Japan	8	3,913	8	7,270	3	1,915	5	6,568	1	1,535
Kenya	—	—	—	—	—	—	—	—	1	1,168
Korea, North	—	—	—	—	1	9,076	—	—	—	—
Korea, South	13	15,410	9	45,770	9	22,423	15	86,636	11	134,382
Kuwait	—	—	—	—	—	—	1	1,501	—	—
Lebanon	4	8,028	6	2,576	6	18,328	4	5,927	2	12,338
Liberia	6	139,668	7	182,573	9	186,791	8	155,064	1	11,045
Malaysia	1	922	4	952	4	6,022	1	3,675	2	5,672
Maldive Islands	1	8,372	3	18,748	—	—	1	10,015	—	—
Malta	—	—	—	—	—	—	—	—	—	—
Mexico	2	31,994	2	2,795	2	10,601	3	7,166	1	560
Morocco	5	1,594	5	7,679	2	7,961	6	174,401	—	—
Nauru	1	—	1	51,543	—	—	—	—	1	948
Netherlands Antilles	—	—	—	—	—	—	—	—	1	1,327
Nicaragua	1	1,428	—	—	1	1,211	—	—	1	1,327
Nigeria	—	—	1	580	—	—	—	—	1	9,504
Norway	1	11,370	—	—	1	642	—	—	—	—

NATIONALITY	1982 No.	1982 G.R.T.	193 No.	193 G.R.T.	1984 No.	1984 G.R.T.	1985 No.	1985 G.R.T.	1986 No.	1986 G.R.T.
Pakistan	—	—	—	—	—	—	1	12,010	—	—
Panama	58	322,278	56	312,026	48	284,750	42	333,710	34	222,139
Peru	1	4,467	—	—	2	8,059	—	—	1	7,121
Philippines	10	11,991	9	20,895	10	14,026	8	13,197	8	8,506
Poland	—	—	2	2,788	—	—	1	1,974	1	3,008
Portugal	1	1,844	2	2,172	1	803	—	—	—	—
Qatar	—	—	—	—	—	—	1	2,904	—	—
Romania	1	88,285	—	—	—	—	1	3,971	—	—
Saudi Arabia	5	26,818	—	—	—	—	—	—	1	1,978
Seychelles	—	—	1	505	—	—	—	—	—	—
Sharjah	1	3,160	—	—	—	—	—	—	1	1,622
Singapore	6	25,116	2	11,539	4	16,282	1	3,278	3	5,843
Solomon Islands	—	—	—	—	—	—	—	—	1	500
South Africa	—	—	1	669	—	—	—	—	—	—
Spain	4	4,433	6	149,988	7	7,285	5	15,123	8	112,345
Sir Lanka	—	—	—	—	—	—	1	3,381	—	—
Sweden	—	—	1	500	—	—	—	—	—	—
Syria	—	—	—	—	—	—	1	1,333	—	—
Taiwan	4	96,840	3	11,625	4	14,363	—	—	3	19,940
Thailand	2	1,978	2	3,550	3	7,223	1	1,329	3	6,381
Turkey	—	—	—	—	2	1,983	2	4,464	—	—
United Kingdom	4	10,081	—	—	—	—	3	2,403	—	—
Uruguay	—	—	—	—	—	—	1	3,562	—	—
U.S.A.	10	69,275	4	45,529	7	63,075	1	519	4	3,623
U.S.S.R.	2	6,439	4	13,026	—	24,229	2	11,688	2	37,405
Venezuela	1	713	—	—	1	3,541	3	7,312	4	16,416
Yemen	—	—	—	—	—	—	1	564	—	—
Yugoslavia	—	—	—	—	3	19,436	2	9,262	1	12,162
Not known	—	—	—	—	—	—	3	4,191	—	—

Index

INDEX 197

International Consultation on
Services to Seafarers
(Rotterdam 1969), 54, 62,
97, 124–9
International Council of
Seamen's Agencies, 54, 56,
123, 136
International Council of
Seamen's Agencies for North
America and the
Caribbean, 50, 124
International Council for
Seamen's Welfare, 109,
132
International Labour
Conference, 129, 132
International Labour Office,
165
International Labour
Organisation, 108, 109,
132, 134
International Maritime
Organisation, 79, 108, 109
International Sailors League,
49
International Shipping
Federation, 79, 108, 109,
132
International Transport
Workers Federation, 84,
108, 109, 114–16, 132;
financial grants, 145, 148,
161
Iran-Iraq War, 59, 84, 93, 156,
159
Ireland, 11

'Jack's Palace', 34
Jackson, Herbert, 113, 114,
162
Jakarta, 105, 180
Janeway, James, 13
Japan, 29, 57, 73, 105, 106,
170
Jarman, Captain Arthur, 157

Jenks, William, 27
Jennings, Samuel, 22
John Paul II, Pope, 175, 182
John, Wing Commander E. C.,
158
John XXIII, Pope, 42, 51, 98,
122, 174, 175
Johnson, J. Augustus, 163
Joncas, Fr. Roland, 106
Jones, Charles, 23

Ken, Dr. Thomas, 21
Kerfoot, Revd. Prebendary
Tom, 55, 62, 124, 127,
128, 130–2, 134, 135
King Edward Nautical School,
34
Kingsley, Charles, 29
'Kisima', 83
Kitagawa, Revd. Dr. Daisuko,
124, 126–8
Kobe Mariners' Centre, 57
Kowloon, 150, 151
Krug, Revd. Bernard, 55,
135–7
Kuijper, Captain Wim, 125,
126
Kverndal, Roald, 19, 24, 140
Kwai Chung, 151–2

labour relations, 82
Labrador, 38
Lambeth Conference (1920),
42, 174; (1988), 179
language difficulties, 7, 88, 91,
92, 94, 96
Laureys, Fr. Alphonse, 57, 124
lay readers, 44, 45, 61, 62
Leij, Jacob, 132
leisure time, 7, 111
Leo XIII, Pope, 29
Liaison Bishops, 104, 180
Liberia, 77
lighter aboard ship vessels, 70
liquid natural gas carriers, 69